A BEAUTIFUL
FRIENDSHIP

Also by Paul Kerensa

So a Comedian Walks Into a Church:
Confessions of a Kneel-Down Stand-Up

Genesis: The Bibluffer's Guide
(Book 1 of an optimistic 66-part collection)

A BEAUTIFUL FRIENDSHIP

A Lent Course Based on
CASABLANCA

PAUL KERENSA
AND ZOË YOUNG

DARTON · LONGMAN + TODD

First published in 2014 by
Darton, Longman and Todd Ltd
1 Spencer Court
140 – 142 Wandsworth High Street
London SW18 4JJ

ISBN 978-0-232-53140-4

A catalogue record for this book is available from the British Library.

Designed and produced by Judy Linard

Printed and bound by Imak Ofset, Turkey

CONTENTS

FOREWORD

Of all the Lent courses in all the world, you walked into this one...

We first saw *Casablanca* together as an ill film. Curled up on the sofa one weekend, one of us was clutching a hot water bottle, the other a mug of flu remedy. It seemed just the right moment to settle in with this tale of love and glory for the first time.

Forties black-and-white films rarely appeal when you're sitting down for an evening's TV. We know a classic film would be a superior choice, but we opt for a soap, a sitcom or a Sandra Bullock rom-com. Of a regular weeknight, most of us will watch *Coronation Street* over *Citizen Kane*, *Gogglebox* over *Gone with the Wind*, and *Holby* over Hitchcock.

So perhaps you've never seen *Casablanca*, and have been waiting for the right opportunity. Perhaps you've been waiting for an 'ill day', like ours. This is a rainy day movie, and one that you're more likely to have seen in umpteen parodies than the real thing (*PK writes:* I saw the Bugs Bunny version *Carrotblanca* a good twenty years before seeing the Humphrey Bogart original.)

Well now's your chance: this is that reason to watch. Even if you're not in a Small Group, gather some friends together and congratulations, you've got a small group. Just one or two others and you have the 'two or three come together in my name' (Matthew 18:20). *Casablanca* has a lot to say about love, hope and sacrifice, and we'll apply these themes to the Christian faith and our lives today.

The film may be over half a century old, but it has timeless status. Its quotable lines, its charismatic leads, and its pitch-perfect scenes have a quality that somehow just works, and lasts. Yet also the wartime context has never been so relevant. As we write this, we are a world at war. The First World War began over a century ago, yet still today's news headlines featured no less than six countries currently engaged in warfare.

We pray that as you read this, many of these conflicts may have found peaceful resolutions. But we are living in a broken world, where new foes appear with new weapons and attempt to draw new battle lines.

Casablanca concerns itself not with frontline warfare, but with the displaced, forgotten refugees. In 2013 the world saw more refugees than at any time since *Casablanca*'s release. More than 50 million people fled their homes that year – mostly from Syria, Afghanistan and central Africa. The countries taking the most refugees are not the wealthy west, but Pakistan, Lebanon and Iran.[1] The visa-seeking refugees of *Casablanca* are still with us today, in vast number.

Whether this will be your hundredth viewing of Rick and Ilsa's wartime encounters, or whether you're a first-timer and have no idea how it ends, then here's looking at you. Find that DVD, and play it, then if you want ... play it again.

Our gratitude goes to our parents Roger and Di and John and Sue for their ongoing support. We also thank the brilliant Small Group leaders at our church, St John's Stoke, Guildford, for their time and dedication, as well as our superb rector Mark Woodward. To those who've read over parts of this book – Bev Colinese, Mike Gibson, Sarah Mould and our curate Kate Wyles – we thank you! Further thanks to Helen and Robin Bateman, David Moloney and all at DLT, and Nick Ranceford-Hadley and all at Noel Gay.

[1] *The Week*, p.9, 28 June 2014

HOW TO USE THIS BOOK

It's simple...

1. This book covers five sessions, each lasting approx 60 – 90 minutes. If you prefer shorter sessions, you'll notice each is made up of two halves ... so you could make the course last ten weeks, of 30 – 45 minute meetings.
2. If you're in a Small Group, great. If you're not, gather a few folks together. ('Round up the usual suspects.') If you can, get a copy of this book for each of them – your church may be able to help you with this.
3. If you're reading this as an individual and not part of a Small Group, that's fine. While the sessions are designed for group meetings, we think you'll get just as much out of it reading through in your own time.
4. Get everyone to watch *Casablanca*. You should be able to get hold of a copy for next to nothing (it recouped its budget some five decades ago, so they shouldn't need to charge full price for a copy).
5. You could:
   - Watch it together
   - Pass it around the group
   - If you prefer, watch it in chunks week-by-week. This book presumes group members have seen the film once through before Session 1 (and we'll suggest short two-minute clips to show again in the meetings as a reminder to fuel discussion). You can watch the film in five instalments – each of approximately twenty minutes, at the start of each session. If you're doing this, we suggest breaking it up to watch as follows:
        Session 1: start – 0:19:50

Session 2: 0:19:50 – 0:46:00
Session 3: 0:46:00 – 1:02:05
Session 4: 1:02:05 – 1:19:40
Session 5: 1:19:40 – end.

6. Invite your members to Sessions 1 – 5, reminding them to familiarise themselves with the film if you're relying on them watching it individually. Even if they've seen the film before, it's worth watching again in the run-up to the course.

7 As a rough guide, you'll see each session runs like this:
   - Ice-breaker
   - Film clip, leading into first half of the session
   - Activity involving pens and paper
   - Another film clip, and the second half of discussion
   - A final thought
   - Closing prayer. We suggest a prayer at the end of each session; you may like your own group prayer-time too, so open or close with our suggestion as you wish.

8. Here's a guide to our short-hand during the sessions:
   Read: Bible verses to be read aloud amongst your group.
   Ask: A short question to be answered out loud.
   Discuss: A slightly longer discussion, to have out loud among your group.
   Reflect: This should be read and reflected upon individually.
   Do: An exercise to be read and acted upon individually.

9. We encourage you to be generous in chairing your group discussions, allowing different points of view, and remembering that there are often no right or wrong answers. Everyone is finding their own way. Try not to let discussions slip, in terms of time or topic. There are some instances where the thinking-points we suggest may unlock backstories of a personal nature, and where possible we've tried to keep these to individual **Reflections**, rather than public **Discussions**. Watch out for anyone feeling pressured to open up in ways with which they are not comfortable. Any follow-on should be in trustworthy, safe and unpressured friendships.

10. There are appendices in the back of the book offering some trivia and other potentially useful nuggets. Each session has lots of discussion points and opportunities for reflection, and while we've suggested timings, feel free to tweak accordingly, and don't be afraid to shorten discussions if you've spent longer on earlier points.

11. Enjoy!

WEEK ONE

'Exit Papers'

'The others wait in Casablanca. And wait ... and wait ...
and wait ...'
Narrator, *Casablanca*

'Be still before the Lord and wait patiently for him; do not
fret when men succeed in their ways, when they carry out
their wicked schemes.'
Psalm 37:7

Leaders' note for Session 1

By the end of this course, we'll have explored that beautiful friendship – between us and our Creator, in Jesus his son. We'll go deeper into what that friendship means, what he's done for us... and what we can do for him.

But let's begin at the beginning, with the broken world that we're all just passing through. We may turn to Christ, but what then? Do we have a one-dimensional belief, or a three-dimensional living faith? We may kneel down and worship but can we also stand up and be counted? In our first session we'll start to address these questions, by looking at the wartime context of *Casablanca* in the unique location of Rick's Café.

As you prepare for your first session, check you are all familiar with *Casablanca*. In amongst the world-famous dialogue, sassy outfits and fedora hats, make sure your group picked up on the key aspects:

- The love triangle. This was Bogart's first romantic lead, and has him unexpectedly confronting his ex, Ilsa Lund. She abandoned him in Paris, and now appears at Rick's with her husband, the freedom fighter Victor Laszlo.
- Rick's lack of knowledge about Ilsa. He spends much of the film unaware of why she stood him up, causing his deep reflection and upset.
- Rick's tough decision between love and virtue. As the holder of two exit visas, Rick is torn between escaping with his old love Ilsa, or helping her husband in danger.
- The film's famous finale at the airport is dependent on Rick's choice of actions.

It is vital to also be aware of the wartime context, as Casablanca represents the many cities flooded by refugees. *Casablanca* was made after the USA had joined the Second World War, but set just before. Here's a brief timeline of relevant events:

- ✦ September 1939: World War II commences as Germany invades Poland.
- ✦ June 1940: The film's flashback in Paris, as the Nazis march in.
- ✦ December 1941: The film's main action takes place in Casablanca.
- ✦ December 1941: Back in reality, the attack on Pearl Harbor, compelling the US to fully enter the war.
- ✦ Summer 1942: *Casablanca* was filmed, amid Allied bombing on Germany and continual conflict between the USA and Japan.
- ✦ January 1943: *Casablanca* on general release. Jewish massacres continued, and the fight back against Germany and Japan took hold.
- ✦ August 1945: VJ Day as the war comes to an end.

Casablanca depicts a world of gambling, smoking, drinking, killing and even accidental adultery. Some Christian websites do down the film for these aspects. Our personal view is that while you can put blinkers up to these elements, the film reflects a broken world. It is a worthwhile watch: just because you witness these acts on screen, you are not condoning them.

The next few pages are for each group member to read before the meeting – so if they've not managed it, perhaps allow a few minutes at the start of the meeting for them to catch up quickly, or encourage them to read it more thoroughly later – maybe not today, maybe not tomorrow, but soon ...

FOR READING BEFORE THE MEETING

This is the beginning of a beautiful Session 1

Everybody Comes to Rick's, the stageplay that became *Casablanca*, was written in note form in a Bournemouth hotel, by teacher Murray Burnett, following European travels in 1938. As Hitler's Reich took hold, Burnett and his wife had glimpsed the beginnings of mass exile, notably in a French nightclub on the Mediterranean, where refugees gathered to hear a jazz pianist.

Five others would contribute to the script before it became the film we now know; in particular twins Julius and Philip Epstein added much of the famous dialogue. But the notion that 'everybody comes to Rick's' is still that key jumping-off point. Refugees, socialites, soldiers and people of all classes end up at Rick's Café. In reality, each one of us finds ourselves in hinterlands like Rick's.

There are times in our lives of waiting in the wilderness. It's appropriate for Lent that we dwell on these moments in our lives. Christianity is born of a wilderness history: Cain banished after killing Abel, the Israelites under Moses, the Jewish people forced out by the Babylonians, and Jesus going there willingly at the beginning of his ministry. It's this that we remember in the approach to Easter.

Casablanca's setting relates to wilderness too. On the edge of the Sahara – one of the most vast physical wildernesses in the world – lies the seaside city of Casablanca. Here in the film, the wilderness continues, only it's a desperate, moral wilderness. Inhabitants are displaced and lost. Most believe they're passing through, but some won't find their way out. Some cave to the police chief's corrupt ways in order to escape. Others flee, or die trying.

Sought-after exit papers can get you to Lisbon, from where you can gain passage to the New World – a place of hope and freedom. We all have times when we long for those escapes: not necessarily geographical escapes, but to be lifted out of our situations. We may not be refugees ourselves, but we can feel trapped: in limbo and wanting to be lifted out, with a chance of a stronger, safer future.

Times of anguish come to all of us in varying degrees, but often even our close friends and family don't know. It can be a lonely place to be. It might be redundancy or debt, or a spiral of addiction. Perhaps you've had times of abandonment, or you've felt wronged by love, like Rick in this film. Prolonged physical or mental illness, or problems conceiving – the list is endless. Life serves up these events, sometimes in bite-sized moments and sometimes in seemingly endless onslaughts. It can occupy your head 24/7, distracting you from the good in life, and numbing you to the passions and opportunities to get out of the rut. But more often than not, these times are characterised by a lack of control. So we wait for an answer, and wait, and wait ...

Soon after we married (and we are married – ignore the different surnames on the cover of this book!), we faced challenges that had been bubbling away for some time. Doctors had told us that children wouldn't happen for us. We were looking into IVF and its less well-known cousin ICSI. It was going to be a long slog. We simultaneously saw doctors at two different hospitals, to increase our chances of hearing radically different suggestions. In the meantime we kept goldfish, as practice. But all along, it was a cloud over the early years of our relationship and marriage. It quickly consumed us – life events like this have that habit of occupying every waking moment, marring the good times and causing great anxiety and hopelessness.

In amongst this, like so many others at the time, Zoë was faced with months of uncertainty over her job, then ultimately redundancy. The worry of 'What next?' was creeping through the nation. It was a time of waiting and wilderness for us, not knowing when we'd be lifted out of it.

There were prayers, there were short-term jobs, and there were hospital visits. Then, totally unexpectedly, we found out that we were expecting our first child. Given our previous expectations, this baby was a miracle, and an answer to so many desperate prayers. Now just a few years later we have a second miracle – so two beautiful children run around our house preventing us from writing this book! In times like this, when events are out of your control, you have to cling to hope. Many people think Christians have all the answers. They don't. Many think they have all the patience and understanding required to get through tough times. They certainly don't.

We've been in situations like these, and known others to be stuck in such moments of desperation. We've seen those who don't know Christ feel there's no Christ to know. We've drifted, and seen others who know Christ begin to drift. In times of crisis, it's very easy to detach yourself from church, from your support network, and from God. We might think we'll just reconnect when life is plain sailing again, but there are dangers of detaching a boat. Overnight it drifts, and you'll wake up to find yourself more lost.

The shifting sands of the Sahara have been likened to waves. Lost travellers have not lasted the expanse of the desert – just a few hundred metres into the desert wilderness, and as the winds continually reshape the landscape, you find yourself with no idea which direction will lead you out. So in life, our tough situations can get tougher if we don't cling to the truths we know, the moral compass we hold dear, and the faith we have built up over time. If your life is good now and your faith is strong, that helps equip you, to steer the course when the going becomes rocky.

This can all sound pretty bleak. But as Christians, the hope we have is in someone *who's been there*. God is not distinct and distant: God lived the life as one of us. God has been there, done that, and has more than enough scars to prove it. Jesus was born into a refugee family, fleeing Bethlehem at word of Herod's troops, with unsettled years in exile. Our God has lived and suffered and died and conquered death. God has even been to that place of wilderness, as preparation for ministry. He fasted, faced temptations, and won out. He came out the other side – which is great encouragement for us to do likewise.

The forty days Jesus spent in the wilderness mirror the forty days Moses spent with God on Mount Zion, when he fasted and was given the Law (Exodus 34:28). The Israelites spent forty years wandering after Egypt, before they could reach the Promised Land (Numbers 14). Some have likened it to the forty weeks that a child grows in a mother's womb. There is a sense of preparation, readiness, equipping, and expectant waiting. It is something we need to go through, in order to come out stronger. In the case of Jesus' time in the desert, it means we can see him as 'the new Adam', as in Romans 5:12 or 1 Corinthians 15:45. In Adam, we faced temptation and failed the trial. Jesus succeeds where man could not. Our hope is rooted in someone who has been through the wilderness, has stared down temptation and won. We can't win on our own. So in times of tribulation, we wait on God, and with God, and for God as our only way out. We don't drift; we cling.

Casablanca shows us a refugee crisis from within recent memory, and we're far from solving this problem in the world today. There are more displaced people today than at any time since the Second World War. All of these stories are echoes of the refugees we hear of in the Old Testament: exiles without a home, persecuted and wandering for countless years. Theirs is a humbling lesson of grace and patience in waiting for God's plan to unfold. Our problems may pale in comparison to true refugees, and their cause should move us, to prayerful action.

Equally, it's not a competition. If you're struggling right now – or know someone who is – then your plight is every bit as important to God. What you're going through, matters. Through this course we'll look at ways to equip and encourage for those rough times.

We're all in this world of wilderness and waiting. At some point or other, everybody comes to Rick's.

SESSION 1

Opening icebreaker

What's the longest you've had to wait in one place for something? e.g. For concert tickets? At a departure lounge? In a doctor's waiting-room? How did you feel and how did you get by?

Some context for you:

- UK drivers spend up to three years of their lives stuck in traffic.
- The average Brit spends five hours and thirty-five minutes per month queuing.
- In 2012, UK government helplines left people on hold for a total of 760 years, according to Fiona Mactaggart MP.
- Naomi Campbell once kept a journalist waiting for just under three hours before appearing for her interview.

Can you beat any of these?

(5 mins)

Trapped in exile

Ask

What does 'exile' mean to you? Do you think of it as temporary or permanent?

Reflect

As we watch a clip of the film's opening, consider how it would feel to be one of those displaced, as we see on screen.

Imagine the uncertainty of your own future safety, and that of your country. We know when World War II ended, but for the cast, crew, characters and original audience of *Casablanca*, nobody knew how long the war would last. Consider how this would feel as you watch the start of the film...

Watch
Show from 0:06:13 to 0:09:32 (introducing Rick's café, and Rick).

(5 mins)

Rick's café houses desperate people of all types, and these new refugees find wartime Europe to be a leveller: wealth does not get you out.

Discuss
Has any of your group longed to escape from a seemingly impossible situation in their life?
How did it feel and what gave you hope?
How did you escape (or maybe you are still there)?

Read
Psalm 34:17 and 1 John 5:14-15. Share any other Bible verses you find a personal encouragement in times when you need to call out to God.

Reflect
The set-up of *Casablanca* shows all kinds of people: rich and poor, honest and devious, happy-go-lucky and serious, carefree and anxious. The characters are all alike in their situation. If we see *Casablanca* and Rick's Bar as a microcosm for our own world, where do you fit in?

- ... Are you trying to get out of a situation?
- ... Is throwing money at the problem not solving the issue for you?
- ... Are you like the wealthy couple looking on ('We hear

very little. We understand even less.')?
- ... Are you trying to help people out of a situation?
- ... Are you burying your head in the sand rather than facing up to the issues?
- ... Are you in possession of 'exit papers'?
- ... Or do you need them?

(8 – 10 mins)

The 1930s – 40s was far from the first time the Jewish people had been refugees. 2,500 years previously, the original Jewish Exile took place, as we read in the books of Daniel, Esther, Jeremiah, Ezekiel and Isaiah. In 586BC, Jerusalem fell, the Temple was destroyed, and the Babylonians conquered the land of Judah. For seven decades, the Jews were a people without a nation. They were scattered and stuck, and they too had to wait, and wait, and wait.

Read
2 Kings 24:10-14 and Jeremiah 29:4, 10-14.

Reflect
These passages include Jeremiah 29:11 – a favourite 'poster' verse, often given in times of needed comfort. Here the Hebrew 'you' ('I know the plans I have for *you...*') is plural, not singular. God's vision and plan is for all of Israel, and it's long-term. In this case, it spans seventy years: a lifetime.

When we look at Jeremiah 29:11 in times of crisis, do we find ourselves hoping for a quick answer, a solution tomorrow? Or can we appreciate the vast plan God has laid out for us, that may span our seventy years or more?

(5 mins)

Do
Take a pen and paper, and note down between five and ten big life moments you've had: a relationship, a house-move, a job offer, a commitment to faith. You may think of

others. Try and go chronologically if you can.

Put a circle around each one – so each becomes like a stepping-stone. Link them together with lines.

Now consider the lines. These are times in between each
life moment. Some of these may signify months or years of
waiting. Were there times of doubt, where you didn't ever
think you'd reach that next stepping-stone – when the job
offer seemed unlikely, or the relationship looked like it would
never happen?

What gave you hope at these times? Perhaps God's plan,
support from friends, outside help, or did you just have blind
optimism? If you could speak now to the 'you' of those
moments, what would you say?

Discuss

Share any findings you have from doing this exercise.

What hope can you give each other for any future moments
of uncertainty?

Commit to praying this week for your fellow group
members and any times of anxiety ahead?.

(7 – 8 mins)

Wilderness and waiting

Ask

Where do we hear of 'wilderness' in the Bible? Try Moses
and the Israelites wandering in the wilderness and Jesus and
temptations in the wilderness.

Watch

Show 0:15:42 to 0:17:00 (Rick and Renault).

OR

Read

Rick says, 'I came to Casablanca for the waters.'
Renault replies, 'What waters? We're in the desert.'

'I was misinformed,' says Rick.

(4 mins)

Casablanca is a wilderness: Morocco's biggest city, sand-wiched between sand and sea. People come to Rick's bar for a way out, for comfort, for guidance.

Read
Isaiah 40:1-3 and Matthew 3:1-3.

Discuss
What's the nearest you've been to a physical wilderness, desert or wasteland? Describe the features of this place.

Now think of times you've been nearest to a *spiritual* wilderness. When in your life have you felt empty, numb, abandoned?

Are there similarities between physical and spiritual wilderness?

(5 mins)

Read
Matthew 4:1-4.

Discuss
How does it help us to know that the Son of Man has been to that wilderness too?

To what extent do you think this was an essential part of Christ's journey and ministry?

When pure good faces down pure evil, and pure good wins out, what does that mean for us in our darkest times?

(5 mins)

Rick's bar is a waiting room of sorts. It's like a departure lounge where all the flights have been cancelled. Some here are actively trying to find their way out; others are worn down and wait passively for their situation to change.

Read
Psalm 27:13-14.

Reflect
There may be situations where waiting is tough in this life (e.g. a difficult job situation, an illness, or waiting for a loved one to find God).

In the Old Testament, there are two main words for 'wait': *Qavah* means to bind together, to look patiently, to tarry or wait, and to hope eagerly. *Yachal* means to hope or wait expectantly. Neither therefore is a passive form of waiting: Hebrew waiting has 'hope' built into the very word.

Does this style of waiting reflect how you're waiting for your situation to change?

Read
Isaiah 40:31 and Romans 8:18-25.

Discuss
Following these readings and reflections, what does it mean to wait on God?

(8 mins)

A final thought on exile

Reflect
In mid-60s AD, Peter wrote to new exiles: not dispersed Jews as in 2 Kings and Jeremiah, but the persecuted and scattered new church. In 1 Peter 1:1 he calls his readers 'God's elect, strangers in the world'. Other translations call them 'exiles'. They are chosen by God for this difficult, tortuous role. The hope that Peter speaks of is not of a political change or geographical return after seventy years, like the Jewish exile six hundred years earlier.

1 Peter 1:3-4 speaks of 'giving us new birth into a living hope through the resurrection of Jesus Christ from the dead,

and into an inheritance that can never perish, spoil or fade – kept in heaven for you.' Verses 8-9 tell us, 'Though you have not seen him, you love him; and even though you do not see him now, you believe in him and are filled with an inexpressible and glorious joy, for you are receiving the goal of your faith, the salvation of your souls.'

This is our ultimate hope. God has a lifetime plan for us, to retrieve us from our present problems and what may feel like an exile. But the bigger plan meant sending His Son to suffer with us and for us. Jesus has been to that wilderness, suffered persecution and death, and he's come through it alive and glorified. God has this way out for us, while all the time, we expectantly wait.

Closing prayer

Heavenly Father,

Thank you for the freedom to express our faith together. Thank you for our homeland and the gift of our relationship with You. Help us to remember those who suffered for our freedom.

Teach us to understand the importance of waiting, and help us to focus on the greater plan you have for us, Father.

Comfort us in our waiting, when we lose hope or feel lost and helpless.

Father, fill us with courage and strength with which to endure any hardship we may face, and help us to remember to be patient in our waiting for you.

We pray through Jesus Christ our Lord,

Amen.

HERE'S LOOKING BACK AT SESSION 1, KIDS

For reading in your own time

The minister who married us, David Bracewell, wrote about waiting: 'It ought to be a creative activity. As we wait things happen, both within us and in the world around us. We discover how refreshing it is to focus on the present moment – the only one we have.'

As we embark on Lent, we wait expectantly for Easter, and perhaps we can lay open our lives in this period, to allow a spiritual MOT. Bracewell concludes: 'Waiting before the cross there is absolutely nothing we can do. In amazement we witness the outpouring of divine love, an act of unmerited grace.'[2]

ZY writes: I have always found waiting very difficult. I remember a time as a child when my younger brother and I entered a model aeroplane building competition. We both decided to use balsa wood, a light material perfect for children under ten to use. After hours of cutting and preparing, I became impatient for my aeroplane to fly. Rather than wait to use the glue my brother was using, I decided in my childish wisdom to use sticky tape – a far quicker option. As I took my plane for its maiden flight, I watched my brother as he continued to patiently glue each small section of his plane together. I revelled in the

[2] *Fifteen Minutes To Wake The Dead* by David Bracewell, pp.113 – 114

fact I would not have to wait for three hours for the glue to dry in order to test my plane, as I threw it into the air only to watch it fall like a cumbersome mass of sticks to the ground. It shattered into pieces, as did my confidence, and I never entered that plane into the competition. After patiently waiting for the glue to dry, my brother admired his plane as it glided gracefully through the air. It looked amazing and flew perfectly. I believe he won that competition. Sometimes all we can do is wait ...

Often the hardest thing about waiting is not knowing if the end is in sight. Statistically, callers on hold are far more likely to give up and hang up if they're not told where they are in the queue. If we're told we're third in line to be answered, or tenth, or even twentieth, we're much more inclined to stick with it.

PK writes: I find rejection tough – don't we all! In my professional life, I'm pitching ideas for sitcoms, radio dramas and books ... and it's never nice (though sometimes it's expected) to get back that short but sweet reply, 'No thanks'. It used to be that at each knockback, I'd find it more and more difficult to muster the energy and positive drive for the next attempt – until I gave myself the mind-set that you just don't know how many tries it will take. Perhaps I'll get a sitcom picked up after five attempted pitches? Maybe it'll take twenty-three? Or a hundred and twenty-three? I have no way of knowing what that magic number is. As we'll see in a few sessions' time, 'Now I know in part; then I shall know fully, even as I am fully known' (1 Corinthians 13:12).

So now I approach each project, aware that I'm making just one more step towards the number that God knows is the right one. At the same time I have to actively trust this could be the one. It's that balance and tension between these two views that means I'm aware each project may not be 'the one', while at the same time being optimistic that it might be.

I used the same philosophy on my love-life when I was in my twenties and thirties! It turned out the love-life magic number was thankfully a bit less than the sitcom script magic number...

ZY writes: ...Good job too!

WEEK TWO

'Of all the gin joints in all the towns in all the world, she walks into mine.'

'I wouldn't bring up Paris if I were you. It's poor
salesmanship.'
Rick to Ilsa, *Casablanca*

'Hear my prayer, O Lord; let my cry for help come to you.
Do not hide your face from me when I am
in distress. Turn your ear to me; when I call,
answer me quickly.'
Psalm 102:1-2

Leaders' note for Session 2

This session uses the second section from *Casablanca*, from 0:19:50 to 0:46:00, if you're playing the film in weekly instalments. Here we're introduced to three of the stars of the film: Ingrid Bergman as Ilsa, Paul Henreid as Victor Laszlo ... and the melody 'As Time Goes By'. This portion of the film contains some of cinema's most famous lines, and is one of the most spoofed scenes in movie history. As a way in, you could find and play an excerpt from the Bugs Bunny version, *Carrotblanca*! (You can find it on the internet, or the special edition *Casablanca* DVD.)

If you want some atmospheric music as your session attendees arrive, may we suggest some light piano jazz? Do encourage your course mates to read the next few introductory pages in advance, or allow time at the start of the session if anyone needs to catch up.

You can also remind your group of the story so far:

Club-owner Rick Blaine is at the cliff-edge of North Africa, where European migrants are desperate to take off to America. Two exit visas have been found and hidden by Rick, who appears unmoved by the anguish around him. Into his life now comes Ilsa, his old flame, and she's requesting 'their song' from the pianist, Sam. For the first time we see emotion from Rick, as he furiously admonishes Sam for playing the banned tune.

Your group should have seen the film – or at least this scene – by the start of the meeting. So they must remember this ...

FOR READING BEFORE THE MEETING

This is the beginning of a beautiful Session 2

In Session 1 we looked at:

Trapped in exile
- People feeling uncertain and frightened about their own future safety and that of their country
- Planning an escape from a seemingly impossible time in life
- Putting yourself in a place of hope when facing doubtful or uncertain times in the future.

Wilderness and Waiting
- Feeling abandoned, rejected and lost in the wilderness
- Waiting in anxious times where there is suffering
- Trusting in God in times of exile; waiting expectantly.

You're walking down the street, thinking about the shopping, plans for the weekend, emails you meant to get back to ... Suddenly around the corner you see your first love. It's the first time in years you've laid eyes on them – and while there may be good memories buried in there somewhere, the main thing you feel is hurt.

This happened to Rick Blaine when he heard 'As Time Goes By', then glimpsed his former sweetheart Ilsa Lund. Abandoned by her at the station as they were due to leave Paris, he never thought he'd see her again. Now here she is.

Of all the gin joints, in all the towns in all the world ... she walks into his.

Memory is a fickle friend. It'll bring up the good times: a song plays on the radio, and your memory will tell you how great that birthday party was, what a fun student you were, how incredible that concert was...

...But then you can be blissfully happy, and out of nowhere your memory will unpack your worst moments. Things you'd filed in your brain but forgotten all about. Corners that no one has shone a torch on for years, nor would they want to. Half a second of a song can be enough for your memory to bring back the summer you were first dumped. A whiff of the wrong food and you're back at an unhappy school day.

PK writes: Personally, I find a certain soap scent has my memory dredging up my days in hospital as a five-year-old. It's a particular brand of antibacterial handwash that reminds me instantly of quaking under the covers in Ward 6CD, awaiting the dreaded Fingerprick Lady, whose sole job was to come and steal blood from children ...

Yes, memory can be the worst best friend ever.

At this point of *Casablanca*, before Ilsa walks in, she is far from Rick's mind. The romantic view might be that he wakes up each day thinking about her, that she never leaves his mind. But the truth is that we do move on ... or we bury our feelings and try to.

So often we try and move on from hurt in our own past without confronting it. The partner may have left, the cause of the upset may never walk into our 'gin joint', but if we hear that song, smell a smell or taste a taste that reminds us of that painful time, then we too are being held captive by it. Like Rick, we're haunted by it, and we're not living life to our full potential by allowing memories to wound us further.

The Christian message on this is simple: forgive. It's harder to put into practice though. The notion of forgiveness is at the very heart of the Christian faith – the word 'forgive' occurs twice in the sixty-six words of the Lord's Prayer. Yet it can be so difficult to put into action. If Rick had managed to forgive Ilsa, not knowing the reason that she left him at the station, then perhaps he could have moved on with his life – but then there'd be no drama and no film!

For our real lives though, the power to forgive is crucial if we are to live our lives to the fullest. It's unfathomable to hear of a mother who can forgive the killer of her child – yet it happens. The deepest regard can be held for victims who can forgive their aggressors, sometimes even facing them in prison.

These are people living out their words of faith. Who can say if we could do the same? It's something that many of us pray on a daily basis: '...as we forgive those who sin against us'. Thankfully many of us may not face severe situations where this is put to the test. But if we can forgive our bullies or anyone else we feel wronged by, then we're doing God's work on this planet.

Jesus said, 'Blessed are the meek', but meek doesn't mean weak. If we are to forgive, with the fierce resolve and determination needed to stand up to our foes, then what place is there for anger and frustration? In this session we'll look at lamenting to God, and its place in a prayer life that has nothing off-limits to God. This session we'll be focusing particularly on Psalm 137, and in the next we'll look at Psalm 139, which will remind us of God's total knowledge of us. God knows our heart and our deepest darkest thoughts (yes, even those ones). We can't hide, so why try? If we lay ourselves bare to God, we can find ourselves having an open conversation with the Almighty – and what can be more exciting than that?!

As we'll see this week, Psalm 137 is written about a suffering people, crying out in the wilderness. They're holding nothing back from God, brutal in their wishes and sorrowful in exile. You might have a faith but that doesn't rewrite your brain so that it's all plain sailing. There's no Christian anaesthetic that numbs us from feeling angry or frightened or vengeful.

John 16:33 gives us Jesus' words: 'In this world you will have trouble. But take heart! I have overcome the world.' So while we may lament to God with all our woes, we can take heart that God hears us, as he heard the people in the wilderness thousands of years ago. We send up our song, and God sends back His Son.

This section of the film has some of the most famous lines not only in *Casablanca*, but in the history of cinema.

We'll hear a 'Here's looking at you, kid.'

We may even hear a 'Kiss me. Kiss me as if it were the last time!'

We'll even throw in a 'Play it, Sam. Play "As Time Goes By".'

One thing we won't hear is 'Play it again, Sam' – because contrary to popular belief, that's not ever said in the film. Far from 'Play it again', Rick's order would be: 'Never play it again, Sam...'

SESSION 2

Opening icebreaker

What songs bring back memories for you, happy or sad? Are there songs that remind you of tough times, that you just can't listen to now?

(3 mins)

Lamenting

Show

Watch from 0:30:00 to 0:33:20 (Ilsa requests their song, Rick storms in).

OR

Read this summary

While her husband Laszlo arranges their escape, Ilsa asks for the jazz pianist to come over. Sam arrives, and even brings his piano – he's on duty after all. Ilsa urges him, 'Play it, Sam. Play "As Time Goes By".' Reluctantly, Sam does so. His boss has expressly forbidden it, and sure enough, in bursts Rick. He hears it, chastises Sam, then sees Ilsa. The memories come flooding back.

(3 mins)

Later, Rick will bellow at Sam to play 'As Time Goes By'. 'You played it for her, you can play it for me!' It pains him, yet now it's the soundtrack to his reminiscence.

Discuss

Why has Rick forbidden the song? Why is Ilsa so keen to hear it?

Is Rick avoiding confronting his painful memories?

Can familiar music be cathartic in dealing with emotional hurt, or will it only make it hurt more?

(5 mins)

Read

Psalm 137:1-6.

Like the *Casablanca* scene, this famous text has found its place in popular culture over the years. The psalm has been reprised and adapted by many, including Liszt, Verdi, Don McLean and of course Boney M! In both 'As Time Goes By' and this psalm, we have powerful music that laments and regrets.

Discuss

What is a 'lament'? Share among your group what the word means to you.

Which parts of the Bible do you think of as 'laments'?

Do you bring your laments to God?

Perhaps they've lost their popularity today, as if they belong three thousand years ago, before we discovered a more grateful way of praying! How do you think lamenting prayers fit into our spiritual lives today?

Reflect

Walter Brueggemann wrote of the lament: 'It is an act of bold faith ... because it insists that the world must be experienced as it really is and not in some pretended way ... It insists that all such experiences of disorder are a proper subject for discourse with God. There is nothing out of bounds, nothing precluded or inappropriate ... Thus these psalms make the important connection: everything must be brought to speech, and everything brought to speech must be addressed to God.'[3]

(7 – 8mins)

[3] 'The Message of the Psalms' by Walter Brueggemann, 1984

Both *Casablanca*'s pianist Sam and the exiled Jews were instructed to play, and in both cases the songs proved too painful. 'I don't want to hear it! Not here!' they cried. Rick's song belonged in Paris, not in Casablanca. The Jews' song felt like it only belonged in Jerusalem. Your songs will have their own place in your life; to hear them elsewhere means facing up to the fears and tears they represent.

Discuss
How does knowing God help to deal with these past fears and tears?

Has your faith been stronger in the tough times, or more fragile?

(3 – 4 mins)

Do
This exercise looks at the power of the psalms as part of our prayer life. Psalm 23 is generally known as the most famous of psalms, and has been used in countless films for characters to face down their worst moments. In *Titanic*, a priest recites it on the tilting ship. In the western *Rooster Cogburn*, Katharine Hepburn's character unblinkingly uses its words to almost turn away bullets. In another western, *Pale Rider*, a girl prays it at a graveside, and between each line of the psalm, she adds a private prayer. We'll echo the latter technique in the following prayer exercise.

Make sure everyone has a Bible. Each person should individually choose a short psalm that talks of trust in God through difficult times: maybe Psalm 23, or perhaps Psalm 8, 11, 16, 63, 142. If there aren't enough Bibles to go around, two people could look at the same psalm.

Privately pray each line, then add a line of your own prayer of something that might be burdening you at the moment. Take a few minutes to commit these words anew to God, and personalise it with what's on your heart. These personalised laments then draw on centuries-old psalms of prayer and praise that still affirm God while sharing our troubles.

Take a few minutes, and then the leader may add the prayer below to draw the prayers together.

Leader
Accept our prayers of praise and lament, Father.
You are God, in the brightest of days and darkest of nights.
Humbly we pray to you, in Jesus' name,
Amen.

(7 – 8mins)

Love and loss

Someone try their best Humphrey Bogart impression: 'Of all the gin joints in all the towns in all the world, she walks into mine ...' This is the Rick Blaine of Casablanca 1941 – frustrated, resentful, railing at the universe for sending Ilsa to his bar.

Try one more Bogart impersonation: 'Here's looking at you, kid!' The Rick Blaine of Paris 1940 – in love and at ease, even in the midst of the Nazis' march on Paris.

Ask
Can you remember a time when a 'memory' has shown up suddenly? Ever bumped into an old flame in the street? Or travelled across the world, only to bump into an old school-friend?

Discuss
It seems like a coincidence that Ilsa has walked into Rick's, of all places.

Does real life serve up such 'coincidences'?

If it's happened in your life, do you see it as chance? Fate? A divine plan?

(5 mins)

Watch

Show from 0:40:35-0:46:06 (Rick's flashback to Paris).

(6 mins)

Ask

How does the old Rick of Paris ('Here's looking at you kid!') compare with the current Rick of Casablanca ('Of all the gin joints...')?

Reflect

Have you ever felt 'abandoned at the station' like Rick? You may have felt wronged by love, by life or by God. Did you express anger or frustration to God, or are you still keeping it inside?

Read

Psalm 137:7-9.

Discuss

This psalm concludes with such anger!

What place does such violent imagery have in a psalm, a song to the Lord?

How do you think God responds to the Jews' railing against him?

How about to Rick's resentment, or to our most pained moments?

(8 – 10 mins)

Perhaps the backbone of Christianity is forgiveness. It's the framework for how we act on our beliefs and move forward.

Read

Ephesians 4:31-32 and Matthew 18:21-22.

Ask

Could Rick have forgiven Ilsa for walking out on him? If he had, what difference do you think that would make in him?

Discuss

To what extent do you believe in the phrase 'forgive and forget'?

Should we do either, or both?

Does the will to do this come naturally to you?

(5 – 7 mins)

Read

John 16:32-33.

Ask

We *will* have tribulation, difficulty, suffering, in this world – we know it and it's been promised! How does knowing Jesus help when we're in that angry, pained place, like the Jewish exiles of Psalm 137 as above?

Read

Romans 8:16-17.

Reflect

Consider whether you deal with moments of anger or abandonment by retreating into yourself, or hurting those around you. Whichever we do, we can hand it over to God and ask for strength. We can pray into these moments, and commit to praying *more* when hemmed in, anxious or abandoned, rather than less.

(5 – 7 mins)

A final thought on love, loss and lamenting

Reflect

White House TV drama *The West Wing* is much-loved in our house. The box set has done at least a couple of circuits, and it doesn't get any better than the 'Two Cathedrals' episode (the clip is available on YouTube if you wish to show it). President Jed Bartlett attends the memorial service of his loyal secretary, Mrs Landingham: the 67 year-old had died in a car collision, on the way back from picking up the first car she'd ever own. After the service, the President takes the unprecedented step of clearing the cathedral. This politician, so used to public meetings and speeches, wanted to privately remonstrate with God about the shockingly unfair death. It is no quiet prayer: Jed Bartlett is demanding an audience with God, in his own house, and he even veers into Latin as the raw emotional protest spills out of him.

We may not have the power to clear a cathedral, or the knowledge of Latin, but we have the power of prayer for our own personal one-to-one with God. Our prayers are of praise, repentance, and intercession. But there are times where we feel abandoned, like Rick at the station, or the Jews in Babylon. It is at these times that we, or others around us, may ask the age-old question: 'Where is God?'

Christianity has a different answer to this than other religions. At Lent we remember Jesus the suffering servant: God's son and God incarnate, yet fully man and fully tortured in death on the cross. He has suffered pain and death as we do... yet he rose through it.

Rick may feel abandoned here, yet at this point in history there was far greater suffering than Rick's: the oppression of the Jews, and the gas chambers to come. It's often asked: Where was God in the gas chamber? We believe the answer is that God was *in* the gas chamber. God suffers with us, and suffers for us. It doesn't deplete our own suffering, but it does transform what's beyond it.

We can lament, and rail against God, because we can't fully understand. But we can rely on God's full and loving knowledge. Romans 8:28 tells us, 'And we know that in all things God works for the good of those who love him, who have been called according to his purpose.'

God has a plan for us, and we'll look more at this in the next session. So it might seem coincidental that 'of all the gin joints in all the towns in all the world, she walked into mine,' but perhaps it's meant to be.

Closing prayer

Loving Father,

You hear us now, as you heard the cries in the wilderness so many years ago.

Help us to remember that you are with us, yesterday, today and tomorrow, at our highest moments and at our lowest ebbs.

When we seek answers, when we do not understand, grant us wisdom.

When we rail against you, when we feel beaten, forgive us Lord and grant us strength.

When we beat our fists at your chest, as a small child would, your loving embrace simply surrounds us, as the most loving of fathers. We thank you that you stand by us when others do not.

We have fallen short, and you love us just the same.

You have sent your Son, who suffered death so that we might live. We know we're not worthy of this, yet your love is greater, and your grace knows no bounds.

As we seek to know you better, grant us patience and mercy, and may we encourage those who do not hear your voice to stop and listen.

We ask these things in your name,

Amen.

HERE'S LOOKING BACK AT SESSION 2, KIDS

For reading in your own time

Time for a Film Studies class.

Some academics have suggested that the imagery of Casablanca is prison-like. Almost every scene is an interior; shots feature shadows of bars or banisters. Often the camera peeks through bars or windows to look at the action, and it's even been suggested that in one of the few scenes outside, in a local market, Rick and Ilsa wear stripes, indicating prison uniforms and inescapable cells.

If Casablanca is a jail, then Rick's sentence is partly self-imposed. He's a prisoner to himself, to the loss and regret that he just can't get over. Rick's past hurt convicts him and keeps him from living a free life. The Rick of Paris – carefree with a bright smile and bright suits – has been replaced by the Rick of Casablanca – in dark suits, playing solo chess, looking out only for himself.

A more recent film that deals with confronting painful past memories is *Philomena*. It tells of a Catholic mother's angst when she tries to track down her son, decades after he'd been effectively sold by the nunnery to which she'd been consigned. It's a compelling and true story that explores the role of forgiveness in confronting past hurt. As Philomena (Judi Dench) searches with a disgruntled journalist (Steve Coogan), the truth they uncover tests the freeing power of forgiveness, as one character manages to forgive, and the other finds only anger. Of course anger is entirely natural given the circumstances ... but with God's help we can be *super*natural in the way we deal with life's obstacles. It's easier said than done, but then isn't that true of everything worth doing?

WEEK THREE

'We'll always have Paris'

'The last time that I trusted a dame was in Paris in 1940.
She said she was going out to get a bottle of wine. Two
hours later, the Germans marched into France.'
Peter Falk spoofing Humphrey Bogart,
Murder by Death

'Now we see but a poor reflection as in a mirror; then
we shall see face to face. Now I know in part; then I
shall know fully, even as I am fully known.'
1 Corinthians 13:12-13

Leaders' note for Session 3

PK writes: I did an acting course at drama school. It condensed three years into one, because it was for postgraduates (who in acting terms are therefore OAPS, and none of us could afford to wait three years before going to seek acting jobs). To fast-track us through the course, the tutors said upfront that they would spend six months breaking us down (getting rid of 'bad habits'!) and six months building us up again. They saw us as half-built houses, where the old bricks needed taking down before the new ones could be laid and rise to completion.

This session marks the half-way point of this short course, and while we've not intended to break anyone down with the first two sessions, this does mark a turning-point as we learn how to build ourselves up. Using Psalm 139 as a basis, we'll reflect on what it is to not only imagine the bigger picture, but to act as part of it. Finally we'll consider how we can be numbed by sadness or when we feel wronged. We can acknowledge when we're in a hole, and we'll claw our way out of it.

It's our second session focusing on a specific psalm. It's apt for the middle of Lent: a time of focus on the forty days of wilderness at the start of Jesus' ministry, and the Passion Week at the end of it. Recall last week's session on psalms as lament, as once again we'll see elements of that here. Do consider that these psalms were used as praise by the suffering exiles, who even in their darkest moments could rely on the Father's majesty.

Have ready some pens and paper, as well as the *Casablanca* DVD (or download, or VHS, depending on the year). It may be helpful to summarise 'the story so far' at the start of your meeting:

Club owner Rick is aghast to see that his old flame Ilsa

has appeared in his bar; she broke up with him via letter as they were to flee the Nazi occupation of Paris. Her husband is freedom fighter Laszlo, who cannot be arrested in Casablanca due to it being neutral territory. Ilsa and Laszlo are seeking exit visas to flee to America, but Captain Renault has been pressured by visiting German officers to ensure that there is no way out for them. Meanwhile, Rick seeks solace in a glass of bourbon at his own bar ...

FOR READING BEFORE THE MEETING

This is the beginning of a beautiful Session 3

So far we've looked at:

1. Trapped in exile
- People feeling uncertain and frightened about their own future safety and that of their country
- Planning an escape from a seemingly impossible time in life
- Putting yourself in a place of hope when facing doubtful or uncertain times in the future.

Wilderness and Waiting
- Feeling abandoned, rejected and lost in the wilderness
- Waiting in anxious times where there is suffering
- Trusting in God in times of exile; waiting expectantly.

2. Lamenting
- Painful memories and sudden reminders
- Facing up to bad experiences
- Opening up to God and expressing ourselves honestly through prayer.

Love and Loss
- Forgiveness of others' wrongdoing
- Handing times of anger and abandonment over to God
- Trusting in God's plan.

Film experts still struggle to pinpoint exactly what it is about *Casablanca* that has made it so enduring. It won the Best Picture Oscar for 1943, yet we aren't as familiar with the Best Picture winners that came before and after, *Mrs Miniver* and *Going My Way*. If it's *Casablanca*'s direction under Michael Curtiz, then why aren't we as familiar with his other work, like *Mildred Pierce* or *Mission to Moscow* (not the *Police Academy* version)? If it's Humphrey Bogart, then why haven't more people seen *The Maltese Falcon* and *The Big Sleep*? The same could be said of the script, the music and so on.

Perhaps what makes it work is the combination of different factors: every element delivers, from direction to script to music to acting to cinematography. Everyone's playing their part, so that the whole motion picture simply works, and it's almost impossible to work out which individual is making it a success. This session we'll be looking at our part in God's big picture. Ultimately it is only God who can step back far enough to take it all in.

There is an amazing photo – worth a Google – taken by astronaut Michael Collins during the Apollo 11 mission of 1969. It features the planet Earth, part of the moon, and – because Collins was on a spacewalk at the time – it also features the Apollo 11 itself. Therefore it's been said that Michael Collins is the only human, living or dead, that is not contained within the photograph. Those yet to be born, and those who have died, are still in the photograph, in different atomic matter. It's impressive. (Pedantic types have pointed out that elements of Collins *are* in the frame if he's ever had a haircut or clipped his toenails. And biblical purists may argue that Elijah, and perhaps Enoch, and one would guess even Jesus, may be exceptions to this ... There's a discussion in itself, but it probably wouldn't get us anywhere!)

God has the only view of all – Michael Collins included – and not just in extreme wide shot, but also in extreme close-up. It's easy to think of God as a bearded man on a cloud, viewing us from afar in the heavens. Michelangelo's 'Creation of Adam' painting has a lot to answer for! God is pictured as some sort of cloud-based Santa, armed with thunderbolts and ready to 'move his furniture' whenever there's loud stormy weather.

This is why so many believers engage with 'the still small voice of calm' of the hymn 'Dear Lord and Father of Mankind', as heard by Elijah in 1 Kings 19:9-13. Christianity is a personal faith. God is the Almighty Creator, yet he speaks to us not from a cloud but from the chair next to us. You could see God as beside you in the car, or as the satnav, or as the car in front that you're following. He's not distant: he's with us, and he's made that literally so by dwelling amongst us in his son Jesus.

These ideas are present in Psalm 139, and in this session we'll look at this poetic reflection on God's knowledge of us. As we look at this psalm, we'll reflect on our own stubbornness to appreciate that there's more to life, and to our current situation, than meets the eye. It's something Rick Blaine would do well to appreciate, as he grizzles his way through Ilsa's visit to his bar, burying his head in a glass of bourbon (in America that means whisky, not biscuits). He blames her for breaking his heart, because he doesn't know what really occurred when she broke up with him.

Knowing only half the story can be dangerous...

ZY writes: When I was a teenager, we got our first proper home computer (jokes about my age are not allowed!). I was as excited as my younger brother, although slightly miffed that I would only get four weeks use out of it before leaving for university. The day came to pick up the new machine. We were delighted. We arrived home, and as soon as it had it been unpacked, my dad and brother took themselves upstairs to 'set it up and test it out'. The door was closed and my mum and I were banned from the study. I was furious! My brother and I had both been introduced to the new-style computers at school, and were surely equally qualified to help set up and test the machine. My mum did not seem at all bothered by this apparent injustice and went downstairs to prepare the evening meal. I remember making my anger over the situation pretty clear to my family. After several unsuccessful attempts of trying to reason with my mum, and gain her alliance for a battle with the males in our family, I embarked on a sole attempt to convince my dad and brother to let me in the study. I was astounded to hear the door of the study lock in front of me. I was enraged. This physical act of exclusion demonstrated to me that I was not wanted or needed in the room. I felt hurt, inferior and angry. I felt that my input in setting up the computer was at least as valuable as my younger brother's contribution and I was flabbergasted at the exclusion. After a lot of door-slamming, yelling and tears, I decided to go for a walk across the fields to cool off. I was gone some time (just to make a point), and arrived home a couple of hours later. To my surprise, I found my whole family waiting for me. They all wore odd expressions on their faces, and I couldn't work out what was going on. Was I in deep trouble for my outburst, or were they dreadfully sorry for what had been a blatant exclusion?

As it turned out, my family had actually purchased not one computer, but two. A desktop for the whole family and a brand new shiny laptop ... for my birthday and to take with me on my impending departure to university. These laptops were quite a thing to have at the time (again, no age jokes!) and the thought of owning one had never crossed my mind ... until now.

As the bigger picture was revealed to me, I emotionally shrunk in size and wanted to crawl under a blanket and not have to face my family. I felt so ashamed, and re-played the whole awful episode back in my head on fast forward.

Needless to say, I apologised to my family for weeks afterwards and I hoped that they forgave me for my awful behaviour (and they did). It is always wise to consider the bigger picture before we act, even if we don't always understand what that picture looks like.

Have you ever seen a picture mosaic, where hundreds of

tiny photos are making up one larger one? Our individual knowledge and perspective is just one of these pictures – we have no idea of the larger plan that God has lined up for us to play a part in.

Psalm 139 is an ode to God's individual knowledge of us – a poem that tries to fathom the unfathomable about God's omniscience. Sometimes we act as if God's knowledge of us is fleeting, checking in on us before focusing elsewhere on a more worthy cause. God can't fully have an eye on our little sins while there's so much else to worry about: a military conflict across the world, or a marital conflict across the street. This psalm tells us that God is fixated on you and me as individuals. God knows our sitting down and our rising up. God knows our words before they're on our tongue. God searches and knows our hearts, including our grievous ways.

God is even described as 'knitting us together' in our mother's womb. When our two children were born, both were greeted with knitted hats or blankets, personally and lovingly created by friends and family. No two hand-knitted items are ever the same, even if they are from the same pattern. Created with love, care and attention, each one has its quirks and fascinations. We found that sometimes the ones that looked unusual, or seemed too big or too small, could be the cosiest. All were loved, because all were made with love.

Let's see the bigger picture. Let us be fully known and fully loved for it.

SESSION 3

Opening icebreaker
This week we're looking at part-knowledge and what it is to be fully known. Your fellow group members may know you well, or maybe not so well – but none of them can know you fully. To open this week, go around the group and ask each person to give one piece of information about themselves that no one else there knows.

We'll start the ball rolling: Paul was in the studio audience for an episode of 1990s TV sitcom *The Brittas Empire*, and Zoë speaks fluent Dutch. Right, over to you.

(5 mins)

Rick sees through a glass, darkly

Show
Watch from 0:46:15-0:48:52 (Rick and Ilsa late at night).

OR

Read this summary
In the bar late at night, Rick has been recalling the Paris of three years ago: when he was in love with Ilsa, and he thought she was in love with him. Ilsa enters the bar ... but Rick doesn't want to hear her explanation. He's got it all worked out – she left him for Laszlo, or perhaps many other men in between.

(3 mins)

Read
1 Corinthians 13:12-13.

Reflect
In the King James Version, 'we see through a glass, darkly' – and in *Casablanca*, Rick literally sees life through a dark glass, staring at it all night in his bar. He thinks he's got Ilsa worked out. He knows nothing since being dumped via letter at a station: this is his part-knowledge. Later in the film we – and crucially Rick – will discover a fuller understanding of what occurred.

Ask
Pick a time when, like Rick, you thought you knew the whole story ... but you didn't. How did you react to your original view of events, and how did you respond when you found out the truth?

Ask
The 1 Corinthians 13 text is part of the well-known 'Love is patient' passage, often read at weddings. Given our lack of full knowledge, how does responding with 'faith, hope and love' help us when we can't see the bigger picture?

(5 mins)

Read
Psalm 139:1-12.

Reflect
God's full knowledge of us is all-encompassing and unattainable, yet this psalm is incredibly personal. God knows when we sit down and when we rise up. How long have you been sitting down for? God knows to the millisecond, and beyond. God knows us to our very core – better than we know ourselves.

Discuss

The idea of someone watching and knowing our every move may not appeal to everybody! How does God's all-loving nature help with this?

Can you imagine wanting to escape God?

The Psalmist wondered if God was escapable... and found God was not. How does this psalm reassure us that God not only knows us, he guides us?

Reflect

When Rick refuses to hear Ilsa's explanation, his stubbornness gets in the way. He doesn't want to hear the truth. Maybe stubbornness is ruling your life. Are you ignoring knowledge and wisdom that is available to you? So often we believe our way is the best way. Yet who knows the full story? God alone knows.

(8 – 10 mins)

Discuss

Discuss Psalm 139:12 '...even the darkness will not be dark to you; the night will shine like the day, for darkness is as light to you.'

What are the implications for us in what seems like *our* darkest hour?

What hope is there when we can't see a way forward?

Reflect

Rick has retreated into himself ... and into a drink. It may be you that's currently in a dark self-reflective time. Or it may be others who are stubbornly shutting the world out, believing they can escape God, and escape the truth that can set them free. Take a few moments to reflect on those we know who would benefit from darkness becoming light, and would know that God's hand will lead them, his right hand holding them.

(5 mins)

You're part of the bigger picture ... let's act like it!

Read
Psalm 139:13-18.

Ask
'... your works are wonderful...' 'All the days ordained for me were written in your book before one of them came to be.' Are all our days wonderful, in our own eyes? What about in the eyes of God who created them?

Discuss
Rick's made a point in the film to stress his neutrality, even though in the past he 'ran guns to Ethiopia', helping those in need in trouble spots across the world.

How do you think part-knowledge of his relationship break-up has affected his attitude to the world?

How has his activist side declined since he feels wronged by love?

(5 mins)

Show
Watch from 0:56:10 to 0:58:25 (Laszlo and Ilsa are offered one exit visa).

(3 mins)

Laszlo remains noble throughout this ordeal. His part-knowledge means risk and uncertainty for both his fate and Ilsa's. This film was made for a wartime audience, partly to encourage ordinary Americans to get behind the war effort. Loyalty, conviction and dedication to the right cause were all important messages to reach the cinema audience.

Read
Proverbs 3:3-7.

Discuss

How we can interpret *Casablanca*'s messages of loyalty and dedication today?

What does the Proverbs passage have to say about relying on part-knowledge, and moving forward with loyalty and faithfulness?

In times of crisis, do our best intentions carry forth into our actions?

(5 – 7 mins)

Read

Psalm 139:19-24.

Ask

These final verses appear harsh and sudden, particularly in contrast to what has come earlier. It is a psalm of anguish from a troubled people. If God were to search our own hearts, would he find the grievous within it?

(3 mins)

Do

Take a pen and paper. Consider what has led to you being here at this exact moment, and write it down. But don't just stop at 'Because John suggested I come' or 'Because I saw a notice up at church'. Go back five or six stages. What led to you meeting John? What led to you being at that particular church to see the notice? Go back far enough to see the earlier decisions in your life that have affected you being here now.

Can you pick out good deeds done by others that have affected these decisions? e.g. Did someone introduce you to a church? Were you set up with a future partner, or given a job opportunity?

(10 mins)

Discuss

Based on this exercise, discuss the good deeds done by others that have contributed to this point in your life.

A practical response

Look out this week for opportunities for good deeds like these. Think of the difference you can make in another's life – a friend or a stranger – if you give an encouraging word, or a generous action. May we look first to our own heart, and realise that however well we know ourselves, God knows us better. God's plans for us are bigger than our own.

(5 mins)

A final thought on being part of a bigger picture

Reflect

We can't see the big picture from our perspective. That was literally true of 24-year-old Lisa Gherardini. Her husband had commissioned an out-of-work artist to paint her, commemorating the birth of their son. When that first dab of oil hit the canvas in Florence in 1503, neither artist nor muse could know that this 'Mona Lisa' would become the most famous painting in the world five hundred years later. Furthermore:

- Sailor George Mendonça embracing a nurse he'd never met on VJ Day in Times Square.
- Mahalia Jackson heckling Dr King in Washington in 1963: 'Tell them about the dream, Martin!'
- Computer user Scott Fahlman suggesting in Sept 1982 that a colon, a hyphen and a close-bracket looked like a smiley face.

None of these could have known the global impact of their actions. We too will never on this earth fully realise the effect our actions have had on others. If God knows our thoughts, has knitted us in our mothers' wombs, and is so inescapable, then what thoughts should we be turning to deeds? What inactivity could we be making active? What causes could we be fighting for, and who could we be encouraging in the coming week? As we go from here, let us make our actions count.

Closing prayer

Heavenly Father,

Though we may not always understand or see the bigger picture, help us to know that our lives are part of a greater plan.

Teach us patience, Father, and in times when we are battling against difficult situations, when we think we know best, help us to put our frustrations and stresses to one side and focus on you.

May we remember to respond with faith, hope and love when we can't see the bigger picture.

Help us to hear you, Father, and let us remember to stop and listen for the still small voice of calm that can be heard speaking gently over the deafening sounds of everyday life.

Thank you that each of us has been created with love and that even our imperfections are perfect to you.

Thank you that we are fully known by you, Father, and that despite our foolish ways, we are forgiven and loved by you, just as we are.

Through Jesus Christ, we pray,

Amen.

HERE'S LOOKING BACK AT SESSION 3, KIDS

For reading in your own time

Some define God as omniscient, omnipotent and omnipresent, as if that sums God up totally. It doesn't convey much about who God is. It's a hurdle for many who don't believe in God. If this deity can see all, know all and do all, isn't that actually... terrifying? There's a reason we all don't apply for *Big Brother*. We don't all fancy our life being glimpsed from every angle.

PK writes: A few years ago, I had a small taste of the *Big Brother* house. There was a Channel 4 show called *Kings of Comedy*: comedians were shut in a Big Brother-style house, and spent each day writing jokes for a live comedy set that night. Everything was filmed by multiple cameras, complete with a Diary Room and a vote-off. I was delighted to be asked to appear on... the non-broadcast pilot for zero money. It meant a week of living in a mocked-up house in a TV studio, with seven other comedians. The living-room led onto a comedy stage where an audience was waiting for us each night, and no one left the house until that audience voted us out.

There were cameras everywhere except the bathroom, filming our every move. Because it was the non-broadcast version – just a test-run for the producers before the *real* stars came in – bits of the house didn't fully work yet, including, it turned out, the lock on the toilet door. I discovered this to my cost, as a fellow comedian/housemate tried to open it: the lock rattled and fell to the floor. The door swung open, revealing me. It was the most embarrassing moment of my life as I saw the seven other comedians gawping at me. Then, from behind the furthest gawper, I saw the wall-mounted camera swivel to what they were looking at – me, on a toilet – and I heard the dreaded whirr as the camera zoomed in from across the room.

Thankfully it wasn't broadcast on Channel 4. Just a couple of hundred behind-the-scenes production crew ever saw it. It's enough, certainly, but I'm grateful it wasn't several million. So how does an all-seeing, all-knowing, ever-present God differ from this *Big Brother* nightmare?

All-loving: that's the missing attribute.

Shame, humiliation, indignity: all those negative emotions I felt are eradicated if you add an ever-loving God to the mix. We have a God who knows us, warts and all – God knows what's in our hearts, our words before they reach our tongues, our fears, and our worst latent sins. And God loves us. The world may point and laugh, but God embraces us.

We write this book as a married couple, and when we married, the vows we said were designed to paint a picture of life at its extremes. Couples commit to loving through sickness, debt and worse.

God has made the same commitment to us, at the moment of our creation. This commitment has another name: 'covenant'. A covenant is not a contract, where a service is offered on the condition that other terms are met. A covenant, whether in your own legal 'will and testament' or delivered by God, is something given freely and unconditionally. So 'love' is God's covenant. God fully knows us and fully loves us (you could add the word 'anyway' to the end of that!), whether our thoughts are in sickness or in health, and whether our morality is rich or poor. There's no escaping God's love, in the highest heights or lowest depths.

God knows all, in a way that we cannot. So in the meantime rather than, like Rick, dwelling on assumptions, let's get busy living for God.

WEEK FOUR

'I Stick my neck out for nobody'

'You know how you sound, Mr Blaine? Like a man
who's trying to convince himself of
something he doesn't believe in his heart.'
Laszlo to Rick, *Casablanca*

'Do what is right and good in the Lord's sight.'
Deuteronomy 6:18

Leaders' note for Session 4

Our penultimate session is once again split in half, with two overlapping sections: on singing out what we believe in, and on tough decision-making. If we can do the former, it will more fully equip us for the latter.

At this point in the film, Rick discovers the truth ... and now he has to act upon it. Maybe as Christians we too reach a point where we discover Jesus as the way, the truth and the life. Now we have to act on it.

We'll do an exercise that explores how passions may have dwindled in our life and faith, and how we need encouragement to re-ignite those flames. Make sure you've got pens and paper ready for this.

We're just one week off the famous final scene, so for those who need a reminder, here's the story so far:

The pressure cooker that is Casablanca is heating up. It's crowded with refugees in need of the difficult-to-come-by exit papers. The only two apparent ways out are either the two visas that Rick seems to be hiding, or, for unfortunate women, coaxing them out of Captain Renault, for a price.

Into this we have Ilsa – Rick's old flame who abandoned him in Paris – and Laszlo – her freedom fighter husband. Rick is reluctant to grant Laszlo an escape, not least because it would threaten his own place in Casablanca as Renault expressly forbids Laszlo's departure. The main reason though seems to be that, as Rick says, 'The problems of the world are not on my shoulders.' He's a man out for himself, despite his own past of freedom fighting. His break-up with Ilsa has left him emotionally scarred, and he's not about to risk his own status to help her husband.

So Laszlo is increasingly hemmed in, the Germans are increasingly confident and the refugees are increasingly desperate. This all comes to a head in the first scene we'll look at this week: The battle of anthems in Rick's café.

FOR READING BEFORE THE MEETING

This is the beginning of a beautiful Session 4

So far we've looked at:

1. Trapped in exile
- People feeling uncertain and frightened about their own future safety and that of their country
- Planning an escape from a seemingly impossible time in life
- Putting yourself in a place of hope when facing doubtful or uncertain times in the future.

Wilderness and Waiting
- Feeling abandoned, rejected and lost in the wilderness
- Waiting in anxious times where there is suffering
- Trusting in God in times of exile; waiting expectantly.

2. Lamenting
- Painful memories and sudden reminders
- Facing up to bad experiences
- Opening up to God and expressing ourselves honestly through prayer.

Love and Loss
- Forgiveness of others' wrongdoing
- Handing times of anger and abandonment over to God
- Trusting in God's plan.

3. Rick Sees Through a Glass, Darkly
- Knowing only half the story
- Responding with faith, hope and love when we can't see the bigger picture
- God's full knowledge of us is all-encompassing and unattainable.

You're Part of the Bigger Picture ... Let's Act Like It!
- Effects of failing to see that there is a bigger picture
- God's plans for us are bigger than our own
- Our role in God's plan for other people's lives.

Have you ever been to a Christian festival, and been blown away by the sung worship? Thousands of people in a giant marquee sing out and sing proud. Some worshippers who would never dream of raising their hands in the air may even do just that (I've been one of them). The band is amazing, the sound is magnificent, glory is given!

Then you come home. It's still the holiday season, so your first service back at church is a little under-attended, perhaps because a coach-load have left to attend the same festival you've just been at. So the few dozen people in a small church building suddenly don't sound the same as the Glastonburyesque praise party you've just experienced. Do you still sing just as strong? Is that hand raised aloft just as it was in that big tent last week?

There's a quirk of large communal singing – football matches, festivals, the Royal Albert Hall – whereby any notes sung out of tune are balanced out. Four men chanting, 'We love you Chelsea, we do...' out of tune sounds abominable (let alone the sentiment! – sorry, Chelsea fans), but a few thousand of them and the out-of-tune notes seem to vanish. It all averages out to sound rousing and hopeful and sometimes joyous (depending how the team are playing). The same can be true of Christian sung worship – that full marquee sounds moving and life-affirming, while a relatively small congregation and a Hammond organ often fails to conjure up the same emotions in us.

Yet we must sing. In our highest highs and lowest lows, whether there are two of us or two thousand, God's with us in all those moments.

ZY writes: The first church I attended as a new Christian was a very large, well-known church in central London with an average Sunday congregation of around two and a half thousand. I immediately joined the choir as I love singing and thought it a good way to meet new friends. Indeed it was! And the singing was fantastic. I loved every minute of every rehearsal and the joy that the music brought me was immense. I experienced closeness to God through the music that I had never encountered before. It was as I sang my heart out, I realised this was the way in which God spoke to me: through music. The joy was magnified on a Sunday when we sang in the services. That feeling of singing in worship to God with thousands of others totally blew me away, and I was quite overcome by the sound, emotion and atmosphere that so many voices could conjure.

I attended a couple of services where I sat with the congregation, rather than the choir, and although the atmosphere was just as amazing, something was subtly different. The next time I sang with the choir, facing the congregation at the front of the church, it struck me. My position in the huge auditorium meant that the voices from the congregation travelled directly towards us: we got the full impact of their singing. It was beautiful, soul-felt and utterly powerful. I found myself thinking that if this was the impact of their worship on me, what an amazing feeling it must be for God to hear people all around the world sing songs of worship. What harmony those sounds would make, and how filled with joy God would be to hear the sounds and see the sights of those God loves in worship. It blew me away.

There were thousands of voices in my experience above. But there was equal beauty in the singing on a small beach, where a few of us clustered around a campfire on a late summer's evening. As the three of us worshipped with our singing, I am sure that this gentler, more understated worship was equally pleasing to God.

We may feel less inspired by a handful of worshippers than a thousand. However, we must remember that both please God just the same. 'For where two or three come together in my name, there am I with them.' (Matthew 18:20)

Later in this session we'll look at Luke 22, when Peter denies Jesus three times. This can be us, when our enthusiasm has waned after those big festival renewals. It's easy to be a Christian with a thousand others around you. The disciples found this on Palm Sunday. Luke 19:37 records that they '...began joyfully to praise God in loud voices ...' as Jesus arrived on the donkey by the Mount of Olives. It must have been quite a festival atmosphere. Just a few days later, these same disciples were scarcely to be seen.

If you read this during Lent, Palm Sunday will be upon us. It's a time of jubilation in the church, but it's also a shaming time. When you think about Jesus' Triumphal Entry, hold with you the clamour of the disciples, and try and carry that enthusiasm through times when the crowd are *not* with you. It's difficult, isn't it?

Whether it's speaking about your faith, or standing up for a cause, the truth is you'll find resistance. People don't want to be convinced; they don't want to change. Whether you're inviting them to a church event, or encouraging someone to get behind a charity, you're effectively knocking on their door, and more than likely they're effectively pointing to the sign they've put up that says, 'I do not buy goods or opinions at this door'.

As such, if you're standing up for what you believe in, you need to be prepared to translate it. The most powerful activists and opinion-changers know how to convey their message both academically and simply. Can you explain your opinion to a child *and* a physicist? Are you ready with an 'elevator pitch' – a snappy three-sentence version of what you believe in? Equally can you wax lyrical for an hour if you had to?

PK writes: When I've been performing at the Edinburgh Festival, we're asked to write a forty-word blurb about the show, as well as a hundred-word version. My press release needed to be longer still, and when selling my show on the Royal Mile, where flyerers promote their show to all and sundry, I needed a show pitch condensed to just a few short seconds to convince people to come and see it. Sometimes I could think of a snappy show plug, but struggled to sell it in a hundred words. Sometimes it would be the other way round. Are you ready to sell your cause to the masses, in shorthand and longhand?

So there will be barriers – many of them put in your way by other people, but some placed by *you.* To live a three-dimensional faith, to stand up for a cause and face the world head on, we're saying that we're willing to step into something new. In taking a stance, we're actually moving forward. It's a march, into the unknown – and our minds don't like the unknown. We've got all sorts of protective impulses that tell us we survive by being safe. So we protect ourselves from anything outside of our comfort zone, and the barriers come up. We tell ourselves we can't go on that march because we're busy that day. We can't invite a friend to an Alpha course, because they'll probably say no. We defer from acting now, because we don't have all the knowledge just yet.

In 1835, Danish theologian Søren Kierkegaard wrote: 'My focus should be on what I do in life, not knowing everything ... The key is to find a purpose, whatever it truly is that God wills me to do; it's crucial to find a truth which is true to me, to find the idea which I am willing to live and die for.' [4]

Have you got one of those?

[4] Journals 1A, Kierkegaard

SESSION 4

Opening icebreaker

This time we're looking at singing out loud and proud. So find a song that everyone knows and can sing along to. Put it on the CD player, mp3 player or other musical amplification device. The object is for everyone to keep singing – in time – as the volume is turned down on the music for fifteen seconds. Give it a go! Can everyone keep singing the right tune? You could even try in twos or threes, or even individually...

(5 mins)

Standing up for our beliefs

Show

Watch from 1:08:10 to 1:11:20 (Rick refuses to sell to Laszlo, then competitive singing breaks out).

OR

Read this summary

Laszlo confronts Rick, begging for the exit papers. Rick refuses, telling Laszlo to ask Ilsa why he won't sell – Laszlo doesn't know that Rick and Ilsa had a past in Paris, though he has his suspicions. On this neutral turf of unoccupied France, Major Strasser leads his men in a chorus of 'Die Wacht am Rhein', and Laszlo defiantly instructs the house band to play 'La Marseillaise'. The band looks to Rick first, and he nods approval. Both sets of singers sing louder and prouder, until the French anthem wins out, with locals singing as tears flood down their faces.

(3 mins)

'Die Wacht am Rhein' is a German patriotic anthem rooted in French-German hostility dating back centuries. The song itself, translated as 'The Watch on the Rhine', speaks of defending German borders, particularly in relation to disputed French-German land around the borders of the Rhine.

'La Marseillaise' is the French national anthem to this day, first becoming so in 1795. It was written by request of the Mayor of Strasbourg, to empower the French against invading troops from Prussia and Austria. Its original title was 'Chant de guerre pour l'Armée du Rhin' ('War Song for the Army of the Rhine') so both songs vying to be heard in Rick's café are actually about protecting the same territory.

To our ears they may sound like two loud songs drowning each other out in foreign languages, but the characters singing know the historical truth behind them. They are singing for their terrain, and for their future. Through opposing anthems, the Germans stake a claim on the land, before the French defiantly claim it back.

Discuss

What public singing have you been involved with, from carol-singing to football chants?

Did you come up against obstacles or opposition?

What emotions did it bring about in you as the singer, or the listener?

(5 mins)

Read

Zechariah 9:9 and Acts 16:22-31.

Ask

How is singing portrayed in these verses?

Discuss

We've looked at two particular psalms over the past two weeks, both of which echo this idea of 'singing for your territory'.

What other psalms echo this idea of singing to stake your

claim? Try Psalms 33, 96 and 117, or many, many others!

Are there psalms that could be said to sing of more than territory? e.g. claiming one's soul, or reclaiming a place in the world?

(5 – 7 mins)

Discuss

Film is at its most powerful when it portrays emotion as in this scene. Discuss other films where characters use music to show defiance. Some suggestions:

- The whistling in *Bridge On The River Kwai.*
- The early songs of *Les Miserables* ('Look Down', 'At the End of the Day').
- The slaves working the fields in *12 Years A Slave*. (There is a notable scene where Solomon Northup resists, then joins the singing with ferocity.)
- The ex-miners' brass band in *Brassed Off.*

Consider non-musical scenes where cinema can show inspiring moments of defiance: standing on the desks in *Dead Poets' Society*, or even Caesar in *Rise of the Planet of the Apes* being mistreated until he's compelled to say his first word: 'No!'

(3 – 5 mins)

It's not just about singing, but about standing up for our beliefs. Cinema simplifies, and we're unlikely to have a scene in our life that sums up rebellion in such a brief yet profound way. These cinematic moments can empower and inspire us, for when we face barriers that we should stand up against.

Read

Daniel 3:13-28.

Discuss

How do you view this passage in light of your earlier discussions on defiance?

Has anyone in the group ever defended a particular cause against adversity?

Is there a time in your life when you've particularly stood up for your Christian beliefs?

What was the reaction?

(8 – 10 mins)

Read
Matthew 5:13-16.

Reflect
We are to be salt, preserving the world, and we are to be light, illuminating its troubled corners. In *Casablanca*, Laszlo has no problem wearing his morals proudly. He will stand up to Nazi officers; he will shout them down. Rick, however, tries to keep a low profile. The best he manages in the singing scene is a nod of approval to the band. Yet even this is a change for Rick. He's coming off the fence, and indicating a will to take sides.

Which are you?

Are you a Laszlo – proudly standing up for what is right? You'd be an activist; you'd have an eye on current affairs, and would act on the injustice you see.

Or are you a Rick – staying neutral where possible, not wanting to cause a scene? Perhaps you do make the odd 'nod to the band'.

Perhaps you're more like Renault, the Vichy police chief – playing sides off against each other, acting only to further your own interests, and fawning over whoever happens to be in power at the time. As we'll see at the end of the film, there is hope even for the Renaults amongst us!

(5 mins)

If you're reading this as a Lent course, by now Easter will be approaching. The cross is on the horizon. First there will be a time of communion and equipping the disciples, and there will be betrayal and denial.

Read
Luke 22:31-34.

Ask
In this passage, is Peter a 'Laszlo', or a 'Rick', or a mix of the two? He wears his heart on his sleeve, but does he truly commit to his cause?

Discuss
Sometimes we think we're doing just great for God's kingdom, yet our actions may reflect something different. If Peter (who ultimately will become the first Pope!) is flawed in this way, how does this frame how we see our own failings?

(3 – 5 mins)

Read
Luke 22:54-62.

Ask
This may be a familiar story to you. But imagine reading it for the first time. Did we expect this denial from Peter, the 'lead' disciple?

Reflect
It's one thing to believe in a cause – it's another to stand up for it against adversity. The story of Peter's denial shows us that even the most saintly of followers falls short. The answer is unlikely to lie with humanity then. Perhaps this passage's legacy is that the importance of Jesus' death and resurrection rests on Peter's failing: we cannot get through it on our own. We may sing strong together, but individually we crumble. We are weak, but in Christ we are strong.

It's crucial therefore that we are able to stand up for what we believe, to sing out proud when we need to. This can apply to faith in Christ, or to a cause on your heart: Where do you see that our world is broken? What injustice urges you to action?

(5 – 7mins)

Torn between love and virtue

Rick is described as 'a man torn between love and virtue'. He is now armed with all the facts: that Ilsa left him in Paris to tend to her ailing husband, long thought dead. Yet even now being fully aware of the back story, he still resists helping Laszlo. He has a dilemma. It's now up to Ilsa to convince him to do the right thing and let Laszlo go.

Show

Watch from 1:16:27 to 1:19:08 (Ilsa begs Rick for the exit visas).

OR

Read this summary

A desperate Ilsa confronts Rick: she needs those exit visas, to ensure her husband Laszlo can escape to America. Rick is the one person who can help Laszlo, yet he does not feel compelled to act. Ilsa tries to appeal to the old Rick, who fought a corner, who took a stance. 'It was your cause too,' she says. 'You were fighting for it in your own way.' Rick replies: 'I'm the only cause I'm interested in.'

(3 mins)

Ask

Rick is the only way out for Laszlo. What is stopping Rick helping him?

Read

James 4:17.

Discuss

In our lives, what stops us doing the right thing? What stops us being Good Samaritans? Consider times you've crossed the road instead of helping. Can you confess any of these to the group?

(3 mins)

Rick has been numbed to inaction. We too can find our passion may have dampened, for a cause, or for our faith. This closing exercise looks at how this may have happened, so distribute pens and paper:

Do

Put your name in a circle in the middle of a sheet of paper. Around it, write some keywords that reflect you in your day-to-day life. What is 'you' on auto-pilot? Note down some chores, some places you may visit, and perhaps some emotions you're likely to feel on a standard day. Once you have five to ten of these, draw a circle around them.

Outside of this circle, imagine life on a day off, or on a short holiday. Write down some keywords that come to mind. Where are you going? Who would you see? What are you doing? How do you feel? Draw another circle around these words.

Lastly, think of your life at its extreme moments. Write down keywords relating to the strongest emotions you've felt. An exhilarating trip you've taken? Or when you've fallen in love? Have you ever volunteered overseas, won a race, or had a rave review for a labour of love? Put a final circle around these words.

Take a moment to admire your handiwork!

For Rick in *Casablanca*, he's been hurt by something in the outer circle, and he's closed off every other emotion and passion in that zone. He's no longer driven by love or justice. Can you relate to this? For some of us, if we're knocked down in our highest moments, we retreat to our inner circle of just getting through each day.

What passions or causes – perhaps in that outer circle of extremes – have you forgotten? We can't live life at extremes all of the time. But are there elements here that can be reignited in your life? Maybe life's just got busy! Or perhaps there has been hurt or woe. Maybe anxiety has crept in, or fear of failure, or loss.

How can you reinvigorate your life to ensure there are elements from that outer circle present in your life? Can you rekindle those passions and causes that you used to fight for?

(7 – 8 mins)

A final thought on love and virtue

Muscle memory is the idea that repetition of a task means we can do it almost without thinking about it – but if you don't use it, you lose it. The same could be said of Rick, and love. He felt wronged by it, and he's now forgotten how to love. It's left him cold.

It means his 'dilemma', between love and virtue, is a little false. We're told in the film that Rick's choice is between these two paths: to choose the love of his life, or to do what's right. The Bible though has a different take on it. 1 Corinthians 13:13 famously says, 'And now these three remain: faith, hope and love. But the greatest of these is love.' Rick needs to work out the most loving action, and that means gaining an awareness of what love really is.

Love is not always about walking off into the sunset with the perfect partner, but about being honest with what's on your heart. He realises that it's not a choice between love *or* virtue, but that love *is* a virtue – the greatest of them all. Love overrides everything, his own happiness included. As the old saying goes, 'If you love someone, set them free.'

Next time, in our final session, we'll look at the sacrificial nature of love, in *Casablanca*'s famous final scene: the beginning of Rick's turnaround, and a beautiful friendship.

Closing prayer

Father God,

We don't always sing your praises as we should. We don't

always stand up for your name as we know we ought. Forgive us when we fall short.

Help us to stand up for what we believe in. Equip us with the whole armour of God: the belt of truth, the breastplate of righteousness, the readiness of the gospel of peace, the shield of faith, the helmet of salvation, and the sword of the Spirit, the word of God.

You, Jesus, are the way, the truth and the life. No one gets to the Father except by you. Help us live this reality in our lives.

Purify our hearts, Lord, and when we find ourselves at a crossroads, we pray for the vision and wisdom to see which way is your way, the loving way.

Grant us humility and boldness during tough choices, and may we give our decisions over to your will, so that we can truly be light of this world and salt of the earth.

To the Father, Son and Holy Spirit, may we sing praises all our days, and may we go forth in love.

In your name we ask these things,

Amen.

HERE'S LOOKING BACK AT SESSION 4, KIDS

For reading in your own time

Rick's tough decision may not be as binary as a choice between love or virtue. But he still has a dilemma. He has two exit visas, three people, a lot of risk in using them, and intense feelings of bitterness, regret and lost love.

When we have tough decisions to take, how do we begin? Here are a few suggestions that may help you see your way through:

1. PRAYER

'Trust in the Lord with all your heart and lean not
on your own understanding; in all your ways
acknowledge him, and he will make your paths
straight.' Proverbs 3:5-6

With any major decision, prayer needs to be at the forefront. Give it over to God. If you know you can move forward in obedience to God's will, and trust that God will protect you, it should ease the stress of the decision, enabling you to keep a clearer focus on the task in hand. 'A problem shared is a problem halved!'

2. TURN OFF UNGODLY INFLUENCES

'Do not conform any longer to the pattern of this
world, but be transformed by the renewing of your
mind. Then you will be able to test and approve

what God's will is – his good, pleasing and
perfect will.' Romans 12:2

Tuned into God yet? Or does the world keep interrupting? Perhaps you're already receiving unwanted advice that only muddies the issue. Zoom in on God and put blinkers up to outside opinion for a moment. There will be time to seek it again if you need external assistance, but it's crucial upfront to rely on Him, rather than the biased opinions of those around you.

3. HOW MANY OPTIONS DO YOU HAVE?

'...the Spirit helps us in our weakness. We do
not know what we ought to pray for, but the Spirit
himself intercedes for us...' Romans 8:26

Isolate the key issues at stake and the possible outcomes. How many options do you think you have? Maybe there's an extra option you haven't considered, so think outside the box. Then consider how you can trim down your list. Perhaps some can be ruled out for practical reasons. What does your decision really come down to? Whether it's moving to the right house, money worries, or having to let down a friend, you may soon find that the problem is simplified to a choice between a couple of options.

4. SCRIPTURES

'All Scripture is God-breathed and is useful
for teaching, rebuking, correcting and training in
righteousness, so that the man of God may be
thoroughly equipped for every good work.'
2 Timothy 3:16-17

Read God's word. Based on your trimmed list of options, you may disregard some if there are core moral issues at stake. Seek biblical guidance on other options where possible. Biblical commentaries may help find your way around. Internet search engines are helpful as a way in, but a broader Bible knowledge is always going to be best.

Perhaps this will help strike through some of your options. What answers glorify God? What answers are quick fixes to save your own skin?

5. SEEK GUIDANCE

'Young men, in the same way be submissive to those who are older. All of you, clothe yourselves with humility towards one another, because, "God opposes the proud but gives grace to the humble."' 1 Peter 5:5

Seek counsel. Church leaders or trusted mature Christians may help talk through any issues, particular any arising from Bible passages.

Sometimes the important thing is to pick a route and go for it. Don't live life like a bit-part in *Jurassic Park* ('Don't move a muscle! Their vision's based on movement!'). Live like an upstream salmon: you swim your hardest or you go backwards.

WEEK FIVE

'Welcome back to the fight'

'I've got a job to do. Where I'm going, you can't
follow. What I've got to do, you can't be any part of.'
Rick to Ilsa, *Casablanca*

'Where I am going, you cannot come. A new
command I give you: Love one another. As I have
loved you, so you must love one another. By this
all men will know that you are my disciples,
if you love one another.'
John 13:33-34

Leaders' note for Session 5

We've reached the final session, which looks entirely at that famous final airport scene. Even if you've not seen it, you'll know it. It's line after line of some of cinema's most celebrated dialogue.

As it's the last week, it would be wise to allow for some follow-up at the end of the course. If group members have questions or issues they want to explore further, it's good if as a small group you can be a place where this can happen. It could be that someone needs help promoting their cause, or help finding a cause. Some may be in a kind of wilderness right now, and might need direction to pastoral teams in the church or elsewhere.

If you've been following this course through Lent, then Easter week will be upon you. In a way then, 'Session 6' is each person's individual reflection on the cross. Society now sees Easter weekend as a time of DIY, furniture sales, or Center Parcs. Easter Day in church can be a curious mix of local non-churchgoers who appear twice a year, and those regular churchgoers who've chosen not to go away for the long weekend. Wherever your group members are for Easter, we wish you a Spirit-filled, Christ-centred, God-blessed time.

FOR READING BEFORE THE MEETING

This is the beginning of a beautiful Session 5

So far we've looked at:

1. Trapped in exile
- People feeling uncertain and frightened about their own future safety and that of their country
- Planning an escape from a seemingly impossible time in life
- Putting yourself in a place of hope when facing doubtful or uncertain times in the future.

Wilderness and Waiting
- Feeling abandoned, rejected and lost in the wilderness
- Waiting in anxious times where there is suffering
- Trusting in God in times of exile; waiting expectantly.

2. Lamenting
- Painful memories and sudden reminders
- Facing up to bad experiences
- Opening up to God and expressing ourselves honestly through prayer.

Love and Loss
- Forgiveness of others' wrongdoing
- Handing times of anger and abandonment over to God
- Trusting in God's plan.

3. Rick Sees Through a Glass, Darkly
- Knowing only half the story
- Responding with faith, hope and love when we can't see the bigger picture
- God's full knowledge of us is all-encompassing and unattainable.

You're Part of the Bigger Picture... Let's Act Like It!
- Effects of failing to see that there is a bigger picture
- God's plans for us are bigger than our own
- Our role in God's plan for other people's lives.

4. Standing up for our beliefs
- Publicly proclaiming our beliefs
- Claiming territory
- Overcoming barriers that prevent us from expressing our beliefs.

Torn Between Love and Virtue
- Doing the right thing and obstructions to this
- Rekindling lost passions
- Love is the greatest virtue.

'You're getting on that plane.' With these words, Rick Blaine changes the ending of *Casablanca* from the one that the audience – and Ilsa – were expecting. Up to this point, Rick seemed fixated on leaving town with his old flame. Instead, he's been hatching a plan for her to leave with her new love, so that they continue fighting for good.

We've looked over previous weeks about standing up for a cause, and it may be that you immediately realised that you're not a Laszlo: a front-of-stage pack-leader. Instead you can be like Rick, an enabler, clearing the path for those who *are* leading the right causes. If your gift isn't in being a mouthpiece, then perhaps you can give a leg up to someone who is. You still have a valuable part to play. You don't have to be Martin Luther King, but would you have given Martin Luther King your plane ticket?

In this final scene, Rick's actions demonstrate that he has chosen love *and* virtue – but that love is a sacrificial love. Numerous films of the day focused on the merits of self-sacrifice, so yes, it was propaganda for the wartime audience. Hollywood was doing its bit to get Americans behind the war effort.

Whatever your views on warfare, the underlying message of self-sacrifice is still valid. We don't need to sign up for the frontline, but we do need to love our neighbour and be prepared to put their needs before our own.

The cast and crew of *Casablanca* have their own painful stories, as many were wartime refugees themselves. The actor S. Z. Sakall, playing Carl the maitre d', lost three sisters to a concentration camp. Perhaps the best example of sacrificial love comes from the man behind the villain of the piece: Major Strasser. Shot by Rick in the final moments of the film, he was played by German actor Conrad Veidt. Veidt was a genuine German officer in World War I, before establishing himself as an international screen actor, flying back and forth between the USA and Germany. When he married a Jewish woman in 1933, he was offered a German loyalty contract by Goebbels, Hitler's right-hand man. If Veidt signed, he would gain an Aryan certificate for his Jewish wife. Instead he refused, and signed onto a pro-Jewish historical film adaptation being made in England. When he received word that a death squad had been sent for him, Veidt and his wife fled for Britain in exile.

War loomed, so he gave his life savings to the British government to help the Allied war effort against the land of his birth. He then moved to Hollywood, where throughout the war he had it contractually enforced that he would only play villainous Nazis. He used his German accent to damage the Nazis on the big screen, risking on-street ridicule in the USA to paint his countrymen in a negative light. Throughout, almost every cent he earned was sent back across the Atlantic to fund Britain's fight. Of Major Strasser in *Casablanca*, Veidt said, 'This role epitomises the cruelty and the criminal instincts and murderous trickery of the typical Nazi. I know this man well – he is a man who turned fanatic and betrayed his friends, his homeland and himself in his lust to be somebody.'

Veidt died a year after filming his *Casablanca* role. His ashes were spread at Golders Green in London, in tribute to his pro-Jewish stance and loyalty to an adopted country that benefitted from most of his wealth.

The rich man asked Jesus how to get to heaven. When the answer came that he should give his money to the poor and follow him, the rich man walked away. He was fixated on heaven, as many of us are. How do we get there? What does it take? But the answer is that it takes sacrifice. If we focused less on the gift of eternal life, and more on what's behind that gift, the sacrifice Jesus has made, we'd see a perfect example of how to live, in order to be people of God.

Sacrifice is at the heart of God's word. Perhaps the most famous Bible verse – 'For God so loved the world, that he gave his one and only Son, that whoever believes in him shall not perish but have eternal life.' (John 3:16) – places sacrifice at the pinnacle of the Scriptures. If God is love, and love is sacrifice, then God is sacrifice: taking our place in the Wilderness. The best we can do is to show gratitude and to learn from it, loving one another wholeheartedly and placing others before ourselves.

Let's say you've moved into a new neighbourhood, and as a moving-in present, someone's given you £37million. How kind! Now what are you going to spend it on? Some on yourself, of course. Some on your family, new neighbours, church, or causes close to your heart? Well, good news! This has happened, to all of us. We've moved into a new neighbourhood, called Earth, and we've each got, on average, 37 million of local currency – or 'minutes' – to spend. Have you been spending your stash of time mostly on yourself? Do you tell yourself you'll give some of these finite minutes away one day, when you've spent more on yourself? In the next week you'll get through ten thousand minutes. What and who are you going to spend those on?

Perhaps you tithe for your church, aiming to spend 10%

of your income on them. Do you time-tithe too? What if you spent 10% of your time working for God? What could that achieve?

There are fresh challenges with this. We may have given our lives to Christ years or decades ago. But a fresh faith is ready to be challenged, and start again if necessary. So it could be that the very idea of Christ as a personal loving companion through your life is new to you. Or it could be that you made a commitment to this friendship with Jesus a lifetime ago. Either way, perhaps you need that new beginning: to look at your life, and be prepared to make changes.

At the end of *Casablanca*, Rick has the fight back in his belly, as does Captain Renault. 'Round up the usual suspects,' he says, showing that he's siding with Rick now after all. Renault tells Rick of a nearby garrison of the Free French – the exiled French government still operating under Charles de Gaulle.

All good films begin with an end (in this case the theft of the exit papers), and end with a beginning. The ending here certainly prompts a new beginning, where Rick and Renault move forward in their fight. It's when you stop sitting on the fence, watching injustices go by, and start going with your gut and your God, that you can move forward.

Wartime theologian Dietrich Bonhoeffer, executed just a fortnight before US soldiers liberated the concentration camp he was held in, said, 'Silence in the face of evil is itself evil: God will not hold us guiltless. Not to speak is to speak. Not to act is to act.'

Let us act, and speak, and keep moving forward.

SESSION 5

Opening icebreaker
Your icebreaker this week is as follows: Throughout the session, look for opportunities to give up something, for someone. It could be giving up your seat, a biscuit, a pen, or something bigger, like a promise of time or assistance in the week ahead. You have until the end of the session to make sure everyone has given at least one thing or made a promise to someone else. Get thinking!

(3 mins)

'Where I'm going, you can't follow'

To the new viewer, *Casablanca* looks like a traditional love story. We're used to these films: boy meets girl, boy and girl are separated by obstacle, boy and girl get back together by the end credits. But here, that's not going to happen. *Casablanca* teaches us that true love requires sacrifice.

Show
Watch from 1:32:10 to 1:33:46 (Rick and Ilsa at the airport).

OR

Read this summary
Rick tells Ilsa that she needs to board the plane with Laszlo. He has a job to do, and she needs to work with her husband to further the cause of the resistance. Rick has got his fight back.

(3 mins)

Ask

Do you think Ilsa would have boarded the plane without Rick's encouragement?

Ask

Rick knew the risk of his own arrest and possible death in letting Ilsa and Laszlo go. What has made him disregard this and put them first?

(4 mins)

Throughout the making of much of the film, the script for this final scene was yet to be written. Ingrid Bergman genuinely didn't know whether her character Ilsa would end up with Rick or Laszlo. Painted into a corner, the writers had to find a way out for their characters, and came up with this final scene: where sacrificial love is the answer.

So often in our lives, if we're stuck, hemmed in with no obvious way out, the way out can be signposted by following Jesus' example: Which way is the most loving? There's a reason that we can be said to 'follow' Jesus – because we often face paths where following someone is the only way through. And he is 'the way, the truth and the life' (John 14:6).

Read
John 13:33-36.

Reflect
Rick almost directly quotes this passage, saying, 'I've got a job to do. Where I'm going, you can't follow. What I've got to do, you can't be any part of.' Like Ilsa listening to Rick, and like Simon Peter listening to Jesus, we find it difficult to fully understand. Sacrificial love is confusing for the person receiving it. Simon Peter and the disciples wanted to follow Jesus wherever he went. Ilsa wanted to stay with Rick regardless of the consequences. And we commit to Jesus, trying to grasp what it means to say that he died for our sins. It's an unfathomable act of love, and we continue deeper into

the relationship, not knowing when we will see him face-to-face. Jesus lays down his life, leaving a sense of mystery, and a commandment that we love each other.

(5 mins)

Discuss

Casablanca's message of sacrifice for the greater good is specifically designed to back the war effort. What is the New Testament's message on self-sacrifice?

Some readings that may help you with this:

- Romans 12:1 - being a living sacrifice
- John 13:37-38 - Peter's will to lay down his life for Jesus
- Luke 10:27 - loving God with all our heart and soul
- Ephesians 5:25 - loving our spouses as Christ loved the church
- 1 John 4, especially verses 8-12 and 19-21 - God's love perfected in us
- 2 Timothy 3:2-5 - a list of what not to be!

(8 – 10 mins)

Read

John 15:13 and 1 John 3:16-18.

Discuss

What does it mean to 'lay down one's life for one's friends'? How can we love 'not with words but with actions and in truth'?

Reflect

We can learn from Rick's story that it's not too late to put these challenges into action. We may have made commitments to Christ years ago, but perhaps our eagerness has been dampened a little. We can follow Rick's example, and turn this around today.

Many of us dawdle through life: neutral, sticking our neck out for nobody. But when the time comes, there is no place for neutrality. War merely hastens this situation, but whether wartime or peacetime, we all eventually reach that place when we're to be held accountable. Are we on the fence, or have we taken a side, and a stance? As Laszlo observes to Rick at this point, 'Welcome back to the fight ... I know our side will win.'

(7 – 8 mins)

Reminder
Have you given up something to someone else this session yet, from the earlier icebreaker? If not, keep thinking!

Do
Break into twos or threes. Each person should think of something that they can do in the next seven days to be a living sacrifice and help someone. It could be giving time (babysitting, lifts, visiting someone living alone, gardening) or giving up something you have that someone else needs (equipment, clothes, food for a food bank, a meal for someone struggling, money to a charity). Commit to it, be held accountable, and try and check back at the next meeting. Write it down if it helps to make sure you do it!

(10 mins)

The beginning of a beautiful friendship

Show
Watch from 1:36:30 to 1:38:15 (Rick and Renault walk off into the fog).

OR

Read this summary
Casablanca ends with Rick's redemption: he has waited in the wilderness, he has loved, lost and lamented, and now he has seen himself as part of the bigger picture, and learned how to stand up for his beliefs. But he is not the only one

seeking redemption. Rick does not walk off into the fog alone; Captain Renault joins him. When he could have turned Rick in, landing himself the arrest to impress the Nazis, he instead surprises Rick by suggesting they both re-join the fight.

From the moment Renault instructs his men to 'Round up the usual suspects' (from which the 1995 thriller takes its name), Rick knows that he's safe. Renault then drops the Vichy-labelled bottle into the bin, showing that he's turning his back on the Vichy government with which he's affiliated. As he walks away with Rick, Renault discusses their disappearance to a Free French garrison, where under the exiled French government they can fight with the Allies.

(4 mins)

Read
Isaiah 43:18-19.

Discuss
Whose journey, out in the wilderness of Casablanca, do you find most compelling? Rick's, from neutral to good, or Renault's, from bad to good? Or maybe even Laszlo's, from good to still good!

Reflect
Some of us may feel allied to Rick – maybe we've been sitting on the fence for too long. Others of us may feel more like Captain Renault – we've been busily scurrying down the wrong path, working for the bad guys, not on the fence but over the other side of it. Are there times in the past where you have been dead to the world, like Rick? Or are there times when you've been alive to the world, but actively allied to the wrong side, like Renault?

(5 mins)

A side-note: We've not mentioned Ilsa's as one of the above stories... because her story doesn't have much of a decisive journey. Casablanca is fairly typical of films of its day, in that the few female characters are perhaps underwritten compared with their male counterparts. Ilsa is told by Rick what to do, and he says that he's going 'to do the thinking for both of us'. She's essentially told who to love by the end of the film!

Today there is an interesting new benchmark to which some are holding films accountable – the Bechdel test. It goes as follows: Is there a scene in which at least two women, with named characters, have a conversation about something other than men? We don't think Casablanca – or many films of the era – quite makes it ....

Read
Ezekiel 36:24-26 and 2 Corinthians 5:16-17.

Discuss
How does saying goodbye to our old selves and our hearts of stone help us move forward with a new heart and spirit?

Reflect and pray
Do you know people who could benefit from parting with their old selves, who need that new spirit in their lives? Take a few minutes to pray into their lives, and ask for their turn-around to begin.

(7 – 8 mins)

A final thought on new beginnings

Read
John 3:1-6.

Reflect
It takes commitment to start again. Nicodemus knew this after his encounter with Jesus. Many may think of Jesus as, like Nicodemus says, 'a teacher who has come from God' (John 3:2) – but does that mean we are living out our relationship with Him? You may have been a Christian for a week or a

lifetime, but you can still recommit to that new beginning.

Churches differ in their opinion on this passage: what it means to be born again, and what it means to be born of Spirit. What we can agree on is the importance of rebirth. Whether you're recommitting through baptism, or waking up with a new zest for what it means to live out your faith, '...no-one can see the kingdom of God unless he is born again.' (John 3:3)

If today's the day you're making that commitment – happy birthday.

Closing prayer

Loving Father,

Help us to remember to follow you in times when there does not seem to be a way out or an answer. We are sorry for times when we know we should speak out or act and we fail to do so.

May we strive to remember each day the enormous sacrifice you have made for us, Lord, in laying down your life in such a profound act of love, so that we may be freed from our sins.

Help us to learn from this greatest sacrifice, and reflect the beauty of your eternal love in our own lives.

May we love each other as ourselves and understand that love may sometimes mean giving up what is most dear to our hearts for others.

Thank you for the chance of a new beginning, the chance to turn back to you.

Thank you for your promise of eternal support and love, your promise of being with us always, to the very end of time.

Amen.

HERE'S LOOKING BACK AT SESSION 5, KIDS

For reading in your own time

Our church does a great thing on the anniversaries of baptisms. Whether you're adult or infant, on the anniversary each year, you are sent a Baptism Anniversary card in the post, plus a message of good wishes in the church news. It's a great way of reminding you that this day is essentially your spiritual birthday. It's the anniversary of your commitment to Christ. So celebrate! And maybe if you've drifted it's a good reminder to refocus.

'Turning to Christ' is one of those phrases, like 'being reborn', that's had a bad rap by the secular world in modern days. Rebirth is scowled at, as a new-fangled Christian concept, even though it's been in the Scriptures for two thousand years. 'I turn to Christ' is muttered by (often non-Christian) godparents, along with mundane mumblings of 'I renounce the devil', as if saying it too loudly will make him hear.

Perhaps you feel that turning to Christ is something you do once in your life, and that you've done it already way back, so that's that ticked off. Or maybe you feel that turning to Christ is something you continually do – not an about-turn, but a fraction of a degree, just tweaking your life into the right direction and focus. Perhaps after the first time, it's not so much turning to Christ as *re*turning to Christ, like a child returns to a parent to say sorry, get forgiveness, and grow in their relationship. For this reason, new beginnings can be for everyone.

In the closing scene Rick says, 'We'll always have Paris.'

Critics say we'll always have *Casablanca*.

Christ says, 'I am with you always, to the very end of the age' (Matthew 28:20). It's the last verse of Matthew's gospel, and so we think it'll serve well to end this book. He's with us always – so do we want to be there for him?

Appendix I

Eleven things you may not know about 'Casablanca'

1. On release, *The New Yorker* reviewed *Casablanca* as 'pretty tolerable'.
2. It's said that Bogart and Bergman didn't seem to get on, and the only witness who ever heard them truly bond said it was over how to get out of this awful movie.
3. Dooley Wilson, playing Sam the pianist, was a drummer. He couldn't play piano, so because the music had to be recorded live, the actual pianist was hiding behind a curtain, in view of the on-camera Wilson, so that he could copy his hand movements.
4. In 2012, the piano in the Parisian flashback sequence sold at auction for $602,500. The piano from Rick's bar, on which Dooley Wilson played 'As Time Goes By', goes on sale at auction as this book goes to print, and is estimated to fetch far in excess of $1m. We're hoping it doesn't, because we've already cleared a space for it ...
5. The plane at the end of the movie was not as far away as it looked. It was a cut-out of a plane, and the actors appearing to fuel it were all of a small height, to force perspective and make it look far away.
6. That famous closing scene came out of nowhere. Due to the war, and financial constraints, the script was not finished when filming started. The film was shot in order, with scenes often written overnight to be shot the next morning. It seems so neat now, but by the end, they'd painted themselves into a corner. Who gets the girl? Film narrative tradition dictates that it should be the leading

man, Rick – it's a romance movie, so Bogart needs to walk off into the sunset with Bergman, surely? But especially in its day, there was little chance of this given Hollywood's moral standards (how they've changed!), meaning that an adulterous relationship could not close the movie. Ilsa was married to Laszlo, so surely *they* needed to leave together? But where does that leave Rick? In the original stageplay script, Ilsa and Laszlo escape and Rick goes to jail for shooting Major Strasser. It wasn't satisfying. To solve this, at one point the scriptwriters nearly killed Laszlo off in the final third of the movie... until thankfully the final scene took shape with its now classic ending.

7. *Casablanca: The TV Series* – why *wouldn't* you want to remake it for the small screen? What could possibly go wrong in recasting and remaking the classic film? Well, a fair amount. It was adapted for television in 1955 as a prequel to the original film, and it lasted ten episodes before being cancelled. Then in 1983, David Soul from *Starsky and Hutch* starred as Rick Blaine in a colour TV adaptation, with Ray Liotta as Sacha. This version fell a few hurdles earlier: it made it to five episodes before TV bosses saw sense.

8. 'Here's looking at you, kid' was not in the original screenplay. Bogart's rumoured to have said it to Ingrid Bergman between takes as she was learning poker.

9. The German version (there was one, eventually) had 'Here's looking at you, kid' translated as 'I look in your eyes, honey'.

10. The last line – and the title of this book – wasn't even written when that last scene was filmed. Bogart dubbed it in months later during editing.

11. Other final lines considered for dubbing included Rick saying to Louis: 'If you ever die a hero's death, heaven protect the angels!' Roll credits.

Appendix II

The gospel according to 'Casablanca' (excerpt)

'I'm going it alone from here.' The teacher chewed a toothpick, and glanced across the gathered men.

The disciples looked at each other, aghast. Simon Peter edged forward towards the man they'd followed through this crazy town. 'But we're here to follow you. Wherever you're going, we're coming with you.'

The teacher stepped to meet Simon, and spoke in hushed tones. 'And you're part of my work – you're what keeps the world going. Do you have any idea what you'd have to look forward to if you came with me?'

Simon looked down at the dewy grass of Gethsemane. 'You're saying this only to make us stay.'

'I'm saying it because it's true,' said Jesus. 'A little while, and you'll see me no longer. A little while more, and you'll see me again, maybe not today, maybe not tomorrow, but soon, then for the rest of your life.'

'But what about us?' Simon pleaded.

'We'll always have Jerusalem,' came his teacher's reply.

'I'll stand by you.'

'I tell you truth. Before dawn breaks, you'll deny me three times.'

Simon scoffed, confused into silence. John, the most beloved of the men, spoke for him, and for all of them. 'We'll all stand by you! We said we would!'

'And you will,' Jesus said to him, then to the rest of them: 'But I've got a job to do. Where I'm going, you can't follow. What I've got to do, you can't be any part of. The problems of twelve disciples may not amount to a hill of beans in this crazy world. You'll weep and lament, but the world will rejoice. Some day you'll understand all this.'

Simon Peter spoke again. 'But, Lord ...'

'Here's looking at you, kids.'

At that, the clattering of armour could be heard beyond the Gethsemane gate, then the sound of a centurion's bellow: 'Round up the usual suspect! i.e. Him!'

Judas arrived first, ahead of the soldiers. He kissed the teacher on the cheek, and stepped back.

The teacher turned to his men, now twelve of them, and said, 'This could be the beginning of a beautiful friendship.'

Some were already edging away, but some were standing firm.